A walk

with CHRIST

through

ETERNITY

Heaven, Hell and The Judgments

By Dawson McAllister and Clark Albright

A Walk With Christ Through Eternity

Shepherd Catalog number 2033
Printed in the United States of America **ISBN 0-923417-45-1**

Second printing—November 1994

Editor and Publication Director: **Wayne Peterson**
Illustrator: **Jay B. Johnson**
Cover Photo: **David Edmonson**
Cover Design: **Charles R. Carpenter**
Computer Graphics: **Rebekah J. Lyon**

SHEPHERD MINISTRIES
2221 Walnut Hill Lane
Irving, Texas 75038
(214) 570-7599

Dawson McAllister

Dawson McAllister is one of America's outstanding youth communicators. He has been a youth pastor, coffee house counselor, author, TV and radio host and friend to thousands of teenagers.

After academic study at Bethel College in Minnesota and Talbot Theological Seminary in California, Dawson became involved in a program for runaways and desperate teenagers that has developed into a nation-wide ministry. His practical experience and spiritual insight make him much in demand as a speaker at assemblies, weekend seminars, conferences and camps. With twenty-five years of ministry to the American student, he was recently awarded an honorary doctorate of ministry degree from Biola University - Talbot Seminary.

A series of prime time TV specials entitled "Kids in Crisis" has enabled him to provide spiritual counsel to teenage youth throughout the nation. And now, an ongoing tool to reach the American teenager is live call-in radio entitled, *Dawson McAllister...Live!* This two-hour weekly satellite program brings troubled, confused teenagers into contact with straight talk and clear Biblical guidance.

Seventeen popular discussion manuals, thirteen video programs and a film series have multiplied his ministry to individuals and small groups.

Dawson lives with his wife and two sons on an historic farm outside of Nashville, Tennessee, where he enjoys breaking and training horses in his spare time.

Clark Albright

Clark Albright is a counselor, youth communicator, and Director of Research for *Dawson McAllister...Live!*, a weekly call-in talk show for teenagers.

Utilizing a passionate love for God's Word, Clark has a penetrating desire to make Christ clear to students and to show Him for who He really is: 'the Way, the Truth, and the Life.' Clark began working with students in Denver Colorado, and broadened his skills at Colorado Christian University where he earned degrees in Biblical Studies, Youth Ministry, and Psychology.

Clark has co-authored with Dawson another teaching manual—*Pack Your Bags--Jesus Is Coming!* In addition to his work at the radio show and writing books, Clark teaches Biblical Studies to junior high and high school students at a local Christian school.

Clark lives with his wife and three children just outside Nashville Tennessee.

A
Discussion
Manual
For
Teenagers

A Walk With Christ Through Eternity

Contents

Use Of This Manual

A WALK WITH CHRIST THROUGH ETERNITY is a study and discussion tool for individuals, one-on-one counseling, youth groups, weekend conferences, seminars and week-long camps.

A WALK WITH CHRIST THROUGH ETERNITY is a teaching manual to challenge the thinking student who is looking for answers. It is an excellent resource for the youth leader who is seeking to develop the faith and commitment of students.

Scripture passages in this manual are highlighted in boxes to call attention to their importance and to make them stand out within the pages. The Bible is our ultimate resource in life and is the heart of this study. Various versions are used to bring out the vital teaching of each passage and to communicate clearly what God says!

The questions are designed to motivate thoughtful discussion, make significant points clearly understandable and to apply Scripture to the individual in current experience.

The planned progression of this study makes it important for the youth leader and the student to follow the chapter topics in succession, at least for the first time.

Introduction

In our culture today it is acceptable to talk about almost anything. But the one thing people talk about less and less is death and the hereafter. Even though we may talk less about it, everyone thinks about it at one time or another. Whether mourning at a funeral or gazing into the stars, we are moved to think about the great beyond.

Thinking about life after death causes us to ask some difficult but exciting questions:

- **Is there life after death?**
- **Will God judge us after we die?**
- **Is there really a Hell?**
- **What will Heaven be like?**

Most Christian students know very little about God's eternal plan. When we are young, death and what happens after we die seems like a million light-years away. Somehow we fail to grasp God's eternal plan for us and the importance of preparing for life beyond this world. The reality is that the decisions we make here on earth determine where we will spend eternity.

God thinks that what happens in eternity and the whole realm of life hereafter is incredibly important. Therefore it would be wise for us—especially in our youth—to think about and wrestle with the truth of eternity. While many teenagers think as little as possible about life after death, God wants us to think about it a lot. We need to know the truth about God's eternal plan and arrange our lives accordingly.

That is what this manual is all about: to help us more clearly understand what God's eternal plan is all about and how we should be preparing for it. So come along for *A Walk With Christ Through Eternity*.

1 Why We Should Study Eternity

1 | Why We Should Study Eternity

Everyone thinks about life after death. There is no escape from asking questions about the hereafter. Whether mourning at a funeral for a lost loved one or a friend, or even gazing into the stars, we are moved to think about the great beyond.

- Can you recall a time you spent thinking about life after death, heaven, hell, and eternity?

Being up in

- What are some questions you have about God's judging of mankind, about heaven, or about hell?

1 | Why We Should Study Eternity

There is a good reason why we cannot completely quit thinking about eternal life. The reason is that God Himself has put the reality of eternity in our hearts. The Bible talks about this in Ecclesiastes 3:11—

Ecclesiastes 3:11 (TLB)
"...But though God has planted eternity in the hearts of men, even so, many cannot see the whole scope of God's work from beginning to end."

As the writer of Ecclesiastes tells us, God has impressed the truth of the life hereafter into our hearts. Ecclesiastes 3:11 also tells us that "many cannot see the whole scope of God's work from beginning to end." Somehow we fail to grasp God's eternal plan for us and the importance of preparing for life beyond this world.

There are several reasons why. One is that our culture is terrified of death or anything that it cannot control. Therefore it does everything it can to block out from our minds thoughts about life after death. Secondly, when we are young, death and what happens after we die seems a million miles away. King Solomon understood this and so he spoke to all the youth of his time when he said in Ecclesiastes:

Ecclesiastes 11:10-12:1 (NAS)
11:10) "So, remove vexation from your heart and put away pain from your body, because childhood and the prime of life are fleeting.
12:1) Remember also your Creator in the days of your youth, before the evil days come and the years draw near when you will say, 'I have no delight in them;'"

Why We Should Study Eternity | 1

It would be wise for us—especially in our youth—to think about and wrestle with the truth of eternity. While many teenagers think as little as possible about eternity, God wants us to think about it a lot. The Bible says in Ecclesiastes 7:2,4—

> Ecclesiastes 7:2,4 (NCV)
> 2) *"It is better to go to a funeral than to a party. We all must die, and everyone living should think about this."*
> 4) *"A wise person thinks about death, but a fool thinks only about having a good time."*

IN THIS CHAPTER, WE WILL CONSIDER SOME OF THE REASONS WHY WE SHOULD SEEK TO UNDERSTAND GOD'S ETERNAL PLAN.

God is an
Eternal
God

Eternity Future • Eternity Present • Eternity Past

Why We Should Study Eternity | *1*

I. IT IS INCREDIBLY IMPORTANT FOR US TO UNDERSTAND GOD'S ETERNAL PLAN BECAUSE GOD IS ETERNAL.

It is impossible to get a glimpse of what God is like without understanding that He is a 'Forever God.' The Bible teaches that there has never been a time or will ever be a time when God has not existed. God's existence is from forever past into forever future. The Bible talks about this in Psalm 41:13—

Psalm 41:13 (TLB)
"Bless the Lord, the God of Israel, who exists from everlasting ages past—and on into everlasting eternity ahead. Amen and amen!"

● According to Psalm 41:13, how long has God existed in the past?

_____

_____

_____

_____

● According to Psalm 41:13, how long will God exist in the future?

_____

_____

_____

_____

1   **Why We Should Study Eternity**

● How long do you think "everlasting eternity" is?

_____

_____

_____

_____

God is from everlasting to everlasting. Because He is everlasting it greatly affects who He is and what His plans are for the future. For example, since God is eternal, He can be far more patient with what is happening in time because God has all the time in the world and then some. The Bible speaks of this in Psalm 90:1-2,4—

Psalm 90:1-2,4 (NIV)
1) *"Lord, you have been our dwelling place throughout all generations.*
2) *Before the mountains were born or you brought forth the earth and the world, from everlasting to everlasting you are God.*
4) *For a thousand years in your sight are like a day that has just gone by, or like a watch in the night."*

● According to Psalm 90:4, what is a 1,000 years to God?

_____

_____

_____

_____

Why We Should Study Eternity

1 | Why We Should Study Eternity

• The Bible says in Psalm 90:4 that a thousand years in God's sight is "like a watch in the night." What does that mean?

_____

_____

_____

_____

In Old Testament times a night was divided into four parts or watches. Thus a "watch in the night" was only three hours long. Because God is eternal, what we think is a long time is really less than a second to God. It is very important to God that we understand that He is eternal. He looks at everything in this world through the eyes of His eternal plan. And if we are even to begin to understand how God thinks and works, we too must look at everything and weigh it with eternity in mind. If it is important to God it should be important to us—and eternity is very important to God. As Jesus said in Revelation 1:8—

> Revelation 1:8 (NIV)
> *"'I am the Alpha and the Omega,' says the Lord God, 'who is, and who was, and who is to come, the Almighty.'"*

II. IT IS INCREDIBLY IMPORTANT FOR US TO UNDERSTAND GOD'S ETERNAL PLAN BECAUSE GOD COMMANDS US TO SET OUR MINDS ON ETERNITY.

God is a loving and wise God. He does not bother us with tens of thousands of commands which are unimportant or which we in His power can not do. When God gives us a command it is because what He is asking us to do is incredibly important and will result in our eternal joy and happiness. There are many powerful commands in the New Testament which God gives us. But one of the most important is found in Colossians 3:1-2—

> Colossians 3:1-2 (NAS)
> *1) "If then you have been raised up with Christ, keep seeking the things above, where Christ is, seated at the right hand of God.*
> *2) Set your mind on the things above, not on the things that are on earth."*

- According to Colossians 3:1 we are commanded to "keep seeking the things above, where Christ is, seated at the right hand of God." What do you think that command means?

_____

_____

_____

God commands us to, by an act of our will, make a life-long effort to seek Christ and do what is important to Him. It is not as though God wants us to simply day-dream about our interpretation of what heaven may be like. No! Heaven is where Christ lives. And so to seek Christ is to seek Him where He is in heaven seated at the right hand of God.

1 | Why We Should Study Eternity

• Paul says in Colossians 3:2 to "Set your mind on the things above, not on the things that are on earth." What do you think he meant?

_____

_____

_____

Our mind greatly influences everything about us. The Bible tells us that what we *think* will dictate how we *live* (Proverbs 4:23). We must not only seek heaven but we must also think the way God thinks. God, who is in heaven, sees everything with eternity in mind. Therefore a person who sets his mind on things above will no longer live as if just this world mattered. We will look at such things as wealth, the world's praise, pride, power and the pleasures of this world the way God does.

Where Our Treasure Is, There Will Our Hearts Be Also

For example, Jesus was very clear about how we should view our possessions with heaven in mind. He said in Matthew 6:19-21—

Matthew 6:19-21 (NIV)
19) "Do not store up for yourselves treasures on earth, where moth and rust destroy, and where thieves break in and steal.
20) But store up for yourselves treasures in heaven, where moth and rust do not destroy, and where thieves do not break in and steal.
21) For where your treasure is, there your heart will be also."

• According to Matthew 6:19, why is it that Jesus does not want us to store up for ourselves treasures on earth?

_____

_____

_____

1 | Why We Should Study Eternity

Jesus clearly taught that whatever treasure we have on this earth is not going to last. Our earthly possessions can be stolen, burned, or destroyed by moth, rats, or any number of things. The Bible clearly teaches that whatever we can see on this earth will never make it into heaven. No matter how expensive the item may be it will not last forever. Jesus warns us not to waste our time storing up things that will not last and which have no bearing on eternity.

● What do you think Jesus meant when He said in Matthew 6:20 "But store up for yourselves treasures in heaven?"

_____

_____

_____

_____

When Jesus talks about treasures in heaven He was talking about more than earthly possessions. He was referring to whatever good that we do on this earth that has eternal significance. For example, when we give our money to feed the poor, love other people in the power of Christ, or tell others about Jesus, we are laying up treasure in heaven. Of course, when we lay up treasure in heaven, we are putting it in a safe place that God keeps for us to enjoy for eternity. Jesus taught that if we spend our time laying up treasures in heaven our heart will be in the right place. And that place is eternity with Christ.

Why We Should Study Eternity | 1

Living For Eternity Rather Than Things Of This World

When we set our minds on things above and lay up our treasures in heaven, we show God that we agree with Him that heaven is what's really important. Our obedience to God's commands makes Him proud of us and prompts Him to give us eternal rewards. The writer in Hebrews clearly points out that part of what makes great men and women of faith is that they lived for eternity rather than the things of this world. The Bible says of these men in Hebrews 11:13-16—

Hebrews 11:13-16 (TLB)

13) "These men of faith I have mentioned died without ever receiving all that God had promised them; but they saw it all awaiting them on ahead and were glad, for they agreed that this earth was not their real home but that they were just strangers visiting down here.

14) And quite obviously when they talked like that, they were looking forward to their real home in heaven.

15) If they had wanted to, they could have gone back to the good things of this world.

16) But they didn't want to. They were living for heaven. And now God is not ashamed to be called their God, for he has made a heavenly city for them."

• According to the passages above, how do we know these men were living for heaven?

_____

_____

_____

_____

1 | **Why We Should Study Eternity**

● According to Hebrews 11:16, how do we know God was proud of them?

_____

_____

_____

_____

God wants to pour out His eternal rewards for those of us who will make living for heaven a top priority in our lives. God longs for each of us to have the attitude of the Psalmists' in Psalm 73:25-26—

> Psalm 73:25-26 (NIV)
> 25) *"Whom have I in heaven but you? And earth has nothing I desire besides you.*
> 26) *My flesh and my heart may fail, but God is the strength of my heart and my portion forever."*

Why We Should Study Eternity

1 | Why We Should Study Eternity

III. IT IS INCREDIBLY IMPORTANT FOR US TO UNDERSTAND GOD'S ETERNAL PLAN BECAUSE LIFE IS SHORT BUT ETERNITY IS FOREVER.

As we have seen, our society hates to dwell on the shortness of life and the cold reality of death. In fact, we would rather think about anything other than those chilling facts. But God is not into denial about the truth. Jesus Himself is truth (John 14:6). And so God in His Word forces us to face up to the harsh truth of life. The fact of the matter is—life is short. Death is coming for all of us. And then we must face the vastness of eternity. In Psalms 90:5-6,10,12, God gives us a dose of reality when He said—

Psalm 90:5-6,10,12 (TLB)
(5,6) "We glide along the tides of time as swiftly as a racing river, and vanish as quickly as a dream. We are like grass that is green in the morning but mowed down and withered before the evening shadows fall.
10) Seventy years are given us! And some may even live to eighty. But even the best of these years are often emptiness and pain; soon they disappear, and we are gone.
12) Teach us to number our days and recognize how few they are; help us to spend them as we should."

In Psalm 90:5-6,10,12 we have colorful descriptions of just how short and painful our lives can be.

● According to Psalm 90:5, explain what you think the Psalmist meant when he said, "We glide along the tides of time as swiftly as a racing river..."

_____

_____

_____

_____

Why We Should Study Eternity | 1

● What do you think the psalmist meant when he said we "vanish as quickly as a dream?"

_____

_____

_____

_____

● Explain what you think the Psalmist meant in verse 6 when he compared our lives to "mowed down" grass?

_____

_____

_____

_____

What powerful word pictures the Psalmist gives us to consider when thinking about the shortness of life. Think for a moment of a person, who cannot swim, caught in a swirling, raging river. No matter how much that person reaches for a slippery rock, kicks in the water, or crys for help, its just a matter of time before that person drowns. The Psalmist likens life to this. No matter what we try to do—whether it is to make money, or be famous, or work out to stay in shape—the inevitable is coming.

Think for a moment about a dream that you've had. You had the dream; but in a couple of hours you have forgotten it. The dream is a blur in your memory. The psalmist says our lives are like that—they vanish as quickly as a dream. Or think for a moment about a time you were cutting grass in the morning when the dew had just dried. The grass is all green and fresh. But by evening that same grass that has been cut is withered. The Psalmist says that life is like this. These graphic illustrations force us to ponder the inevitable—that our lives are very, very, short.

1 | Why We Should Study Eternity

A Short and Painful Life

The Psalmist tells us just how short our lives really are. He says in Psalm 90:10—

> Psalm 90:10 (TLB)
> *"Seventy years are given us! And some may even live to eighty. But even the best of these years are often emptiness and pain; soon they disappear, and we are gone."*

- Do you agree with what the Psalmist said in Psalm 90:10?

_____

_____

_____

_____

It is amazing that the Bible is so accurate. Most people don't live past eighty years. At the same time those eighty years are often full of heartbreak. There is a saying that has been around for a long time. It goes "life's hard and then you die." The Bible teaches that this is true. Because life is so short and full of incredible pain, the Psalmist tells us what we should do.

> Psalm 90:12 (TLB)
> *"Teach us to number our days and recognize how few they are; help us to spend them as we should."*

Why We Should Study Eternity | *1*

How do you think we should spend our short days? One of the most important ways that we should spend our lives here on our very short journey through life is to prepare ourselves for eternity. King David also understood the brevity of life and how futile it is apart from God. His description of life and his reason to live should also be our reason to live. He said in Psalm 39:5-7—

Psalm 39:5-7 (NIV)
5) "You have made my days a mere handbreadth; the span of my years is as nothing before you. Each man's life is but a breath.
6) Man is a mere phantom as he goes to and fro: he bustles about, but only in vain; he heaps up wealth, not knowing who will get it.
7) But now, Lord, what do I look for? My hope is in you."

Like David, we should know that when we put our faith in God, He not only gives us meaning to life on this earth but in knowing Him there is the assurance of a life that lasts forever. This life that lasts forever with God will be a life of joy, purpose and without pain. King David said it so well in Psalm 23:4-6—

Psalm 23:4-6 (NIV)
4) "Even though I walk through the valley of the shadow of death, I will fear no evil, for you are with me; your rod and your staff, they comfort me.
5) You prepare a table before me in the presence of my enemies. You anoint my head with oil; my cup overflows.
6) Surely goodness and love will follow me all the days of my life, and I will dwell in the house of the Lord forever."

Why We Should Study Eternity | *1*

IV. IT IS INCREDIBLY IMPORTANT FOR US TO UNDERSTAND GOD'S ETERNAL PLAN BECAUSE CHRIST DIED TO SETTLE THE QUESTION OF WHERE WE WOULD SPEND ETERNITY.

God in His love and wisdom understands the pitiful predicament of mankind. On the one hand, there is no way we can stop from thinking about death and the great beyond. And yet on the other hand we apart from God's help are terrified of eternity. Any person who has ever been to a funeral for someone who does not know God, knows of the pain and emptiness of death and going into eternity without God. And the writer of Psalm 89 understood this pain. The Bible tells us that he cried out to God in Psalm 89:47-48—

> Psalm 89:47-48 (TLB)
> *"Oh, remember how short you have made man's lifespan. Is it an empty, futile life you give the sons of men? No man can live forever. All will die. Who can rescue his life from the power of the grave?"*

- Do you know of anyone who's life has been rescued from the power of the grave?

_____

_____

_____

- Why is the power of the grave so awesome?

_____

_____

_____

1 | Why We Should Study Eternity

God has understood our predicament and in His love has moved to help us. His plan was to send His own Son to die on the Cross for our sins and rise again. The only one who has ever completely broken the power of the grave is Jesus Christ. Christ did all of this so that those who believe in Him would have a wonderful life after death.

In John 3:16, the most popular verse in the Bible, God simply explains His plan so that we need not worry about life after death but rather can face eternity with total confidence.

> John 3:16 (NIV)
> *"For God so loved the world that He gave His one and only Son, that whoever believes in Him shall not perish but have eternal life."*

- According to John 3:16, whoever believes in Christ shall not perish. What do you think "shall not perish" means?

_____

_____

_____

To perish does not mean to go out of existence. In this verse, perish means to live a life apart from God. When a person dies and does not know Christ, they do not simply cease to exist. Their soul leaves their body and exists in a whole new spiritual realm. Yet those who never come to Christ will spend eternity apart from God, which the Bible calls Hell.

- According to John 3:16, what do you think eternal life means?

_____

_____

_____

Why We Should Study Eternity | 1

For those of us who believe in Christ we are promised to have eternal life. There is no greater gift. Eternal life means more than simply life forever. Even people who don't believe in God have life forever. Eternal life for those who trust Christ means a life of quality and goodness beyond anything we can now imagine. When Jesus Christ died on the Cross it was the most painful experience any person in eternity has ever had to endure. But God in His love was determined to give us eternal life. He knows that life forever with Him is the greatest gift anyone can have. The Bible speaks of this in 1 John 4:9—

> 1 John 4:9 (TLB)
> *"God showed how much He loved us by sending His only Son into this wicked world to bring us to eternal life through His death."*

IN CONCLUSION

God thinks that what happens in eternity and the whole realm of life hereafter is incredibly important. He wants us to know about life after our earthly lives. And so He has an eternal plan. God the eternal one wants us to think about Him and His plan. He understands that life is short and apart from Him has no hope. God has moved Heaven and earth to send His Son, Jesus Christ so that we might have eternal life. It would be wise for us therefore to know as much as possible about eternity. That's what this manual is all about: to more clearly understand what eternity is about and how we should be preparing for it even now as we live on this earth. So come along for a walk with Christ through Eternity.

> Revelation 1:18 (NIV)
> *"I am the Living One; I was dead, and behold I am alive for ever and ever! And I hold the keys of death and Hades."*

2 | The Rapture & The Glorious Transformation of our Bodies

A s we saw in Chapter 1, understanding and preparing for Eternity is the most important thing we as Christians can do. The question is: When does Eternity begin? What will happen that will trigger us into a whole new eternal spiritual world as opposed to the every-day world in which we now live? In a real sense, Eternal life is a gift that is given to us the moment we put our faith in Jesus Christ. In John 5:24, Jesus said:

> John 5:24 (NIV)
> *"I tell you the truth, whoever hears My word and believes Him who sent me has eternal life and will not be condemned; he has crossed over from death to life."*

So in a way, Eternal life with God begins the moment we put our faith in Jesus. We also know that a person enters the Eternal spiritual realm when that person dies. Jesus taught us that when a person dies, he does not go out of existence but rather into a whole new life in the eternal world. Jesus said in John 11:25-26—

> John 11:25-26 (NIV)
> *25) "...I am the resurrection and the life. He who believes in me will live, even though he dies;*
> *26) and whoever lives and believes in me will never die...."*

2 | The Rapture & The Glorious Transformation of our Bodies

Yet, God has set a time when a new kind of Eternity for all people alive or dead will begin. That moment will be one of the most incredible moments of all time. It is at that moment when a Walk with Christ through Eternity begins.

> **IN THIS CHAPTER, WE WILL DISCUSS CHRIST'S RETURN FOR HIS FOLLOWERS AND THE AMAZING TRANSFORMATION OF OUR BODIES SO THAT WE WILL BE EQUIPPED FOR ETERNITY.**

The Rapture & The Glorious Transformation of our Bodies | 2

I. CHRIST WILL RETURN FOR HIS FOLLOWERS AT THE RAPTURE.

At the very heart of what is important about being a Christian is the belief that Christ will return for His followers. The apostle Paul talked about this when he said to the church in Thessalonica—

---

1 Thessalonians 1:9b-10 (NIV)

9b) "...They tell how you turned to God from idols to serve the living and true God,

10) and to wait for His Son from heaven, whom He raised from the dead—Jesus, who rescues us from the coming wrath."

- According to 1 Thessalonians 1:9b-10, what three things should Christians be doing?

_____

_____

_____

_____

2 | The Rapture & The Glorious Transformation of our Bodies

All of creation seems to be waiting for that moment when Christ will return. Christians call this great moment in time—the Rapture. The apostle Paul spoke in detail about the Rapture in 1 Thessalonians 4:16-18—

---

1 Thessalonians 4:16-18 (NIV)

16) "For the Lord himself will come down from heaven, with a loud command, with the voice of the archangel and with the trumpet call of God, and the dead in Christ will rise first.

17) After that, we who are still alive and are left will be caught up together with them in the clouds to meet the Lord in the air. And so we will be with the Lord forever.

18) Therefore encourage each other with these words."

• According to 1 Thessalonians 4:16 what remarkable things will take place at the Rapture?

_____

_____

_____

_____

• What happens to the Christians who had already died before the Rapture?

_____

_____

_____

_____

The Rapture & The Glorious
Transformation of our Bodies

● What will happen to the Christians who are still alive at the time of the Rapture?

_____

_____

_____

_____

Paul tells us that something amazing will take place. The bodies of Christians who have died and those of us who are still living will immediately be caught up in the clouds to be with Christ. It is at this moment that those Christians who have died and those living will receive their new Eternal bodies.

2

The Rapture & The Glorious Transformation of our Bodies

II. AT THE RAPTURE, WE WILL BE GIVEN AMAZING NEW RESURRECTION BODIES EQUIPPED FOR ETERNITY.

It is incredible to think that at the Rapture all those who have believed in Christ will get new bodies. When we think about the Rapture we are forced to ask some hard questions about what will take place. For example, What will our new resurrection bodies be like? The apostle Paul himself asked a similar question in 1 Corinthians 15:35—

---

1 Corinthians 15:35 (NIV)
"But someone may ask, 'How are the dead raised?' With what kind of body will they come?"

The apostle Paul asked a question that everyone wants to know the answer to: What will our resurrection body be like? That's a very important question; after all, we will live forever in this new body. God does not go into great detail in His Word about this new resurrection body. He does however, give us a glimpse of this great eternal creation that will one day be ours. So what kind of body will it be?

A. Our Eternal Resurrection Body Will Be Far Greater than the Bodies We Now Have.

God originally created man's earthly body to be perfect. It was His plan that humanity be an awesome statement about Himself and His creativity. But when mankind rebelled against God, God judged him and now we all must pay the consequence of sin, which is death. Because all of mankind is under God's judgment, our physical bodies have suffered greatly. They are subject to sickness, weakness, and most of all, death. But one day these judged bodies of ours will be made new again. Paul talks about this in 1 Corinthians 15:42-44—

2 | The Rapture & The Glorious Transformation of our Bodies

> 1 Corinthians 15:42-44 (TLB)
> *42) "In the same way, our earthly bodies which die and decay are different from the bodies we shall have when we come back to life again, for they will never die.*
> *43) The bodies we have now embarrass us, for they become sick and die; but they will be full of glory when we come back to life again. Yes, they are weak, dying bodies now, but when we live again they will be full of strength.*
> *44) They are just human bodies at death, but when they come back to life they will be superhuman bodies. For just as there are natural, human bodies, there are also supernatural, spiritual bodies."*

- According to 1 Corinthians 15:42-44, describe what our judged earthly bodies are like.

_____

_____

_____

_____

- According to 1 Corinthians 15:42-44, describe what our future bodies will be like.

_____

_____

_____

_____

OUR WEAK BODY PROJECT

Think back to a time when you were very sick. How did it feel to have a less than perfect body? Write down your thoughts.

_____

_____

_____

_____

From Weak, Dying Bodies to a Glorious Body

As we have seen, these judged, earthly bodies of ours are weak, sickly, decaying and dying. When we die, our corpse will be put into the grave broken and lifeless. But the Bible tells us one day Christ will transform these frail or lifeless corpses into glorious bodies. Paul tells us of this amazing transformation in Philippians 3:20-21—

Philippians 3:20-21 (NIV)
20) *"But our citizenship is in heaven. And we eagerly await a Savior from there, the Lord Jesus Christ,*
21) *who, by the power that enables Him to bring everything under His control, will transform our lowly bodies so that they will be like His glorious body."*

2 | The Rapture & The Glorious Transformation of our Bodies

● According to Philippians 3:20-21, what do you think is the meaning of the phrase "our lowly bodies"?

_____

_____

_____

_____

● According to Philippians 3:20-21, we will have a "glorious body" like Christ. What do you think "glorious body" means?

_____

_____

_____

_____

A Glorious Body

The Bible tells us that we will truly have an amazing body. The apostle Paul called it a "glorious body." "Glorious" can be defined as brilliant, spectacular or awe-inspiring. Our glorious bodies in Heaven will be an awesome display of God's creative ability. So great are these bodies that they will be modeled after the glorious resurrection body of Christ. For example, this body will be so great that it will move at the speed of one's thought. All a person in heaven will have to do is think of a destination and one will be there. Still another awesome quality of this body will be its ability to move through objects or matter without causing damage to the object or the body. Yes, our new resurrection bodies will truly be glorious.

The Rapture & The Glorious Transformation of our Bodies

B. Our Eternal Resurrection Body Will Be like Christ's.

What an incredible moment it will be—when we see Jesus. His awesome power will change our bodies. In the twinkling of an eye we will be given a body like Christ. It will not be a body fashioned after the greatest sports heros or the world's best models or even an angel. It will be a body like Jesus Christ's body.

> 1 John 3:2 (NIV)
> *"Dear friends, now we are children of God, and what we will be has not yet been made known. But we know that when He appears, we shall be like Him, for we shall see Him as He is."*

- According to 1 John 3:2, when we see Christ we will be like Him. What do you think this means?

_____

_____

_____

_____

We will have a body like the body of the resurrected Jesus Christ. But what kind of body will that be? There is much we do not know about Christ's resurrected body. However, the Bible does give us a glimpse of the resurrected Christ.

1. Our Eternal Resurrection Body will be Real and Recognizable.

Our Eternal Resurrection Bodies will not be made up of some spiritual vapor or ghostlike form. Because these new bodies will be made like Christ's resurrection body, they will be real and recognizable. The Bible talks about Christ being real and recognizable after His resurrection in Luke 24:36-40—

The Rapture & The Glorious Transformation of our Bodies

The Rapture & The Glorious Transformation of our Bodies

Luke 24:36-40 (NIV)

36) "While they were still talking about this, Jesus himself stood among them and said to them, 'Peace be with you.'

37) They were startled and frightened, thinking they saw a ghost.

38) He said to them, 'Why are you troubled, and why do doubts rise in your minds?

39) Look at my hands and my feet. It is I myself! Touch me and see; a ghost does not have flesh and bones, as you see I have.

40) When He had said this, He showed them His hands and feet."

- According to Luke 24:37, what was the reaction of the disciples when they saw Christ?

_____

_____

_____

_____

- According to Luke 24:37-40, how do you think the disciples were able to recognize Christ?

_____

_____

_____

_____

The Rapture & The Glorious Transformation of our Bodies

- According to Luke 24:38-40, what did Christ do to prove He had a real body and was not a ghost?

_____

_____

_____

_____

When Christ first appeared to His disciples after the resurrection, they were so frightened they thought they were seeing a ghost. The last time they had seen Him—His body was beaten and battered beyond recognition and nailed to the Cross. His lifeless body was placed in a tomb. The disciples were absolutely shocked that Christ was alive. The fact that Christ suddenly appeared in a room with locked doors gives us some clue as to the powerful nature of His resurrection body. This new resurrection body was not limited by physical matter or space. Christ could disappear and reappear somewhere else in an instant. He realized they were blown away by His sudden appearance in a new resurrection body. He offered proof that it was indeed Him, resurrected from the dead. He had the disciples touch Him to see that He, like they, had flesh and bones.

As we have discussed, our new heavenly bodies will be like Christ's resurrection body. Therefore, our heavenly bodies will be real, recognizable and powerful bodies of flesh and bone. The disciples clearly recognized Jesus Christ in His resurrection body. For example, the Bible tells us about Christ appearing to His disciples after His resurrection early one morning by a lake. The apostle John tells us that no one had to ask 'Who are you?' for they knew it was Jesus:

> John 21:12 (NIV)
> *"Jesus said to them, 'Come and have breakfast.' None of the disciples dared ask Him, 'Who are you?' They knew it was the Lord."*

2 | The Rapture & The Glorious Transformation of our Bodies

● According to John 21:12, how do you think the disciples knew it was Jesus?

_____

_____

_____

_____

The disciples were able to recognize Christ's resurrection body because it was very similar in appearance to Christ's body before His death. The disciples had spent three years with Christ. In that time they must have seen Him thousands of times. They knew who He was. When He arose from the dead in His new body, they recognized Him. We too will be recognizable in our new resurrection bodies.

In his book, *Heaven: The Last Frontier*, Grant Jeffrey talks about our new resurrection bodies:

> Although our bodies will be transformed, we will still retain our human characteristics that will make us recognizable to those who have known us on earth.... There may be some choice in our appearance. Those who died after eighty or ninety years of life may choose to have a new body issued to them in the appearance of a (younger) mature adult. A child who dies at the age of three may choose a more mature body in Heaven. Some may choose to have their body express the same physical appearance as the day they died. Whatever the outward expression, our intellectual and spiritual nature in Heaven will be that of a mature saint having the complete faculties of an adult so that we may enjoy all that Christ has prepared for us.... Kids will know their parents. Parents will know their babies or children who died at a young age.... What a glorious prospect! On that wonderful future day in which believers will rise to meet Christ in the air, our joy will be multiplied by the greatest family reunion in history.[1]

_____

[1] Grant Jeffrey, *Heaven: The Last Frontier* (New York: Bantam Books, 1990), 46-47.

The Rapture & The Glorious Transformation of our Bodies

2. Our Eternal Resurrection Body will have a Great Mind.

Most people want to know: What kind of mind will we have in Heaven? Will it be the inferior mind we have now? Will it be a mind that sometimes forgets and cannot understand or answer the hard questions of life? Anyone who has ever studied for finals or achievement tests knows there is a limit to our minds' ability. And many of us experience 'burnout' (mental exhaustion) at least once a year. Sin affects our minds in much the same way it affects the rest of our bodies. It causes them to be frail, weak, and less than what God designed them to be. However, Paul tells us that one day we will have great minds:

> 1 Corinthians 13:10-12 (NCV)
> *10) "But when perfection comes, the things that are not perfect will end.*
> *11) When I was a child, I talked like a child, I thought like a child, I reasoned like a child. When I became a man, I stopped those childish ways.*
> *12) It is the same with us. Now we see a dim reflection, as if we were looking into a mirror, but then we shall see clearly. Now I know only a part, but then I will know fully, as God has known me."*

● According to 1 Corinthians 13:10, Paul says, "When perfection comes, the things that are not perfect will end." What do you think Paul means when he says "perfection will come?"

_____

_____

_____

_____

2 | The Rapture & The Glorious Transformation of our Bodies

Because of sin here on this earth, nothing is perfect. Yet Paul tells us of a time when perfection will come. This "perfection" will begin the day we see Jesus Christ face to face in our new eternal resurrection bodies.

- According to 1 Corinthians 13:12, what are the limitations of our minds now?

_____

_____

_____

- According to 1 Corinthians 13:12, how much will we know in Heaven?

_____

_____

_____

The Bible says that "when perfection comes, the things that are not perfect will end." This includes our minds. At long last, our minds will be all that God had originally intended them to be. Finally, our minds—the source of so much pain and heartbreak—will be made perfect.

Scientists believe that the average person uses only 5 to 7% of their mental capacity. It is believed that even a genius like Einstein utilized only 10% of his mental potential. But imagine how wonderful our eternal resurrection bodies will be when we will be able to use 100% of the mental talent God gave us.

OUR GREAT MIND PROJECT

List below some questions of things in our world that you would like to know more about. (an historical event, a science subject, etc.)

_____

_____

_____

_____

List some questions about some issues in your own life that you would like to know the answer to.

_____

_____

_____

_____

What an exciting time we are going to have in Heaven with our new minds. It will take an eternity to learn all the things God wants us to know. Yet, we will never tire of learning. Every bit of knowledge will give us even more joy. At long last we will have an awesome mind.

The Rapture & The Glorious Transformation of our Bodies

3. Our Eternal Resurrection Body will be Full of Love and Joy.

Apart from Jesus Christ, perhaps God's greatest gift to us is our emotions. God gave us powerful emotions so that we might fully experience Him. Yet because of sin, we have lost our capacity to fully enjoy and feel all that God wants us to feel. Our rebellion towards God has caused our emotions to be twisted and confused. But in Heaven, our mind and body will be full of healthy emotions. The Bible talks about in Psalm 16:11 the great joys we will have in Heaven —

Psalm 16:11 (NCV)
"You will teach me how to live a holy life. Being with you will fill me with joy; at your right hand I will find pleasure forever."

- According to Psalm 16:11, what do you think David means when he says "Being with you will fill me with joy?"

_____

_____

_____

_____

No one has ever totally been filled with absolute joy. But when we get our new resurrection bodies, we will have the capacity to take in more emotions and more joy than we could ever begin to imagine.

• According to Psalm 16:11, what do you think David means when he said, "at your right hand I will find pleasure forever?"

_____

_____

_____

_____

There will be no boredom or depression in Heaven. Whatever our pleasures will be—they will last forever. We have just begun to experience the powerful emotions we now have. But in Heaven our new resurrection bodies will be able to receive and keep healthy feelings forever and ever.

When we see Jesus Christ face to face, our total being will be consumed with His love. Every relationship we've ever had with other believers will suddenly be perfect. This means that we need not fear Heaven, for it will mean relationships full of love. The joy of knowing God intimately and seeing His new creation will fill us with joy. No wonder King David said as He thought about eternity—

> Psalm 16:11 (NCV)
> "You will teach me how to live a holy life. Being with you will fill me with joy; at your right hand I will find pleasure forever."

The Rapture & The Glorious Transformation of our Bodies

4. Our Eternal Resurrection Body will have New, Powerful Eyes.

One of the most fragile but important parts of our body is our eyes. Without them, our world becomes a sea of darkness and confusion. Yet at the same time, these very eyes are so incredibly fragile. For example, they can only adapt to so much light. If one stares at the sun for any length of time, blindness occurs. There is no brighter being in eternity than Christ Himself. The Bible says that Christ will light up the heavens with His presence. In fact, God is so bright that we cannot look on Him and live. In Exodus 33:18-19a; 20-23, we are told an amazing story of how Moses longed to look into the eyes of God. Moses wanted to see God's face.

Exodus 33:18-19a; 20-23 (NIV)
18) "Then Moses said, 'Now show me your glory.'
19) And the Lord said, 'I will cause all my goodness to pass in front of you, and I will proclaim my name, the Lord, in your presence....
20) But,' he said, 'you cannot see my face, for no one may see me and live.'
21) Then the Lord said, 'There is a place near me where you may stand on a rock.
22) When my glory passes by, I will put you in a cleft in the rock and cover you with my hand until I have passed by.
23) Then I will remove my hand and you will see my back; but my face must not be seen.'"

● What was it that Moses wanted to see?

_____

_____

_____

_____

The Rapture & The Glorious Transformation of our Bodies

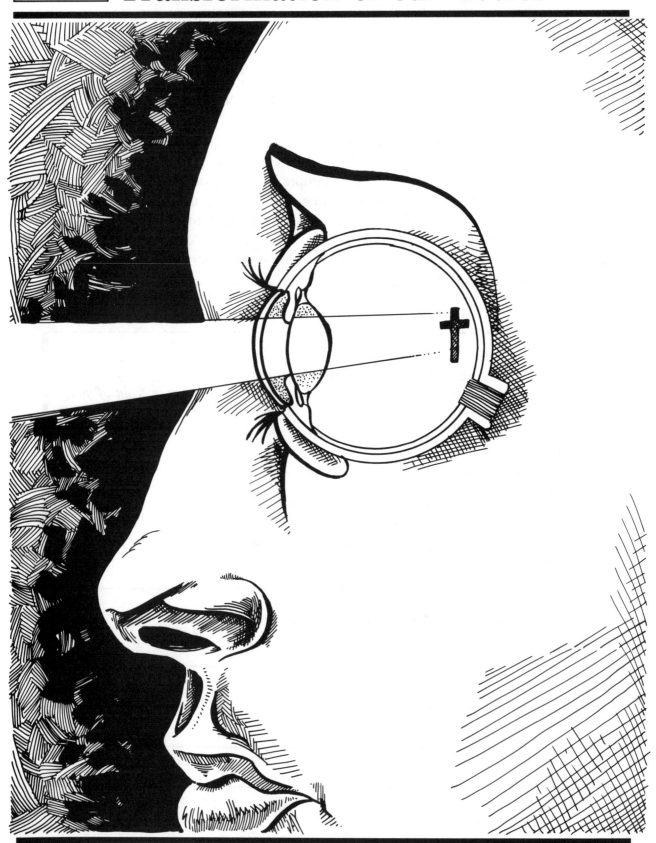

The Rapture & The Glorious Transformation of our Bodies

● According to v. 20, what did God say would happen to anyone who saw His face?

_____

_____

_____

_____

● Why do you think God would not let Moses see His face?

_____

_____

_____

_____

God is Holy. His holiness is beyond anything we have ever experienced. His brilliant light radiates His true holiness. Because we have sinned, our whole being, including our eyes, cannot take in the light of God. Yet in Heaven, the Bible is clear—we will see God face to face. What amazing eyes we will have in our resurrection body. We will be able to see more clearly, with more color and perfection than we could ever begin to imagine. But most beautiful of all, these eyes will be equipped so that we will be able to look into the very face of God and see what no person has ever seen before. The Bible talks about this when it speaks of Heaven in Revelation 22:3b-5—

Revelation 22:3b-5 (NCV)
3b) "...The throne of God and of the Lamb will be there, and God's servants will worship Him.
4) They will see His face, and His name will be written on their foreheads.
5) There will never be night again. They will not need the light of a lamp or the light of the sun, because the Lord God will give them light. And they will rule as kings forever and ever."

IN CONCLUSION

It is easy to get discouraged when we look at our frail human bodies. Yet, God has given us hope beyond our wildest dreams. The Bible tells us that one day in the twinkling of an eye our bodies will be changed into a body like Jesus Christ's. It will be a body that will be so wonderful that we will be thrilled to know that it will be ours forever. One day soon we will be ready for Eternity, equipped with a body that only God can create.

The Rapture & The Glorious Transformation of our Bodies

NOTES

_____

_____

_____

_____

_____

_____

_____

_____

_____

_____

_____

_____

_____

3

The Judgment Seat of Christ & The Marriage of the Lamb

3 The Judgment Seat of Christ & The Marriage of the Lamb

Great things happen when Christ comes back for those who believe in Him. The Bible tells us that at the moment of the Rapture all those who have believed in Christ, both the dead and the living, will be given new resurrection bodies that will last forever. At that same moment, something else will take place that will truly amaze us—we will meet Christ face to face in the clouds! Seeing Christ will be one of the greatest moments in eternal history. But of course, we won't stay with Jesus hovering in mid-air. Instead, we will move on to Heaven, for there is much more of God's plan that we must enter into with Him. The Bible teaches that when we get to Heaven all Christians will stand before the Judgment Seat of Christ, and we will also experience the Marriage of the Lamb. Since there is much confusion over these two great events it is important that we understand them. Most assuredly they await us in the near future.

> **IN THIS CHAPTER WE WILL TRY TO UNDERSTAND THE INCREDIBLE EVENTS THAT WILL TAKE PLACE AT THE JUDGMENT SEAT OF CHRIST AND THE MARRIAGE OF THE LAMB.**

3 | The Judgment Seat of Christ & The Marriage of the Lamb

I. IT IS VERY IMPORTANT THAT WE CLEARLY UNDERSTAND THE INCREDIBLE EVENTS THAT WILL TAKE PLACE AT THE JUDGMENT SEAT OF CHRIST.

It is easy to become fearful and anxious when one thinks about going before a judge. Yet there is no escaping the fact that every Christian will stand before the ultimate judge—Jesus Christ. There will be a day of reckoning when Christ will sit on His judicial bench and we will stand before Him, face to face.

A. What Is the Judgment Seat of Christ?

At the Judgment Seat of Christ the good things every Christian did for Christ will be tested. These good works will be tested to see what motives the Christian had in doing them. At the Judgment Seat of Christ, rewards for what was done in the past will be given and new jobs for future work will be assigned. Paul talks about this in 2 Corinthians 5:10—

> 2 Corinthians 5:10 (NIV)
> *"For we must all appear before the **judgment seat of Christ**, that each one may receive what is due him for the things done while in the body, whether good or bad."*

The Judgment Seat of Christ & The Marriage of the Lamb

- According to 2 Corinthians 5:10, the apostle Paul said that "we must all appear before the judgment seat of Christ,..." What do you think "the judgment seat of Christ" is?

_____

_____

_____

_____

- Paul went on to say "that each one may receive what is due him for the things done while in the body". What do you think "the things done while in the body" means?

_____

_____

_____

_____

Paul says, "we must all appear before the judgment seat of Christ,..." The Judgment Seat of Christ will not be an examination to determine a person's destiny. When Paul used the word "all," he was referring to all those who had put their faith in Jesus Christ. But what do you think he meant when he said, "judgment seat of Christ?" When Paul wrote of the Judgment Seat of Christ (2 Corinthians 5:10), he no doubt had the Greek Olympic games in mind. To the Greeks, sporting events were extremely popular. The greatest sporting event of that day was the Greek Olympic games held just outside Corinth. In the arena where the games were held, there was a raised platform where the judge of the games sat. There he rewarded not only the winners, but also all the contestants who participated. It is that seat that Paul had in mind when he said "we shall all appear before the judgment seat of Christ." It is there that every Christian's good works will be judged and rewards given.

The Judgment Seat of Christ & 3
The Marriage of the Lamb

B.   At the Judgment Seat of Christ Only a Christian's Good Works Will Be Judged.

There are Christians who are terrified because they have been told that somehow at the Judgment Seat of Christ everything they've ever thought or done will be brought to light and revealed to all. Therefore they live in constant dread of standing before Christ. These Christians mistakenly think that every sin they ever did on this earth will be exposed for all the world to see. Yet the Bible is clear: God has forgiven our sins and refuses to remember them anymore.

> Hebrews 8:12 (NIV)
> *"For I will forgive their wickedness and will remember their sins no more."*

In fact, it is very clear that the sins that we do on this earth have all been paid for at the Cross and can not be brought against us when we see Christ. The apostle Paul talks about this in Colossians 1:21-22—

> Colossians 1:21-22 (NCV)
> *21) "At one time you were separated from God. You were His enemies in your minds, and the evil things you did were against God.*
> *22) But now God has made you His friends again. He did this through Christ's death in the body so that He might bring you into God's presence as people who are holy, with no wrong, and with nothing of which God can judge you guilty."*

3 | The Judgment Seat of Christ & The Marriage of the Lamb

• According to Colossians 1:22, because of what Christ has done for us at the Cross, what kind of spiritual condition will we be in when we stand before God's presence?

_____

_____

_____

_____

God calls those who believe in Christ "justified". This means that we are as pure as His Son Jesus Christ. Since God has declared us as pure as His Son Jesus Christ, there is nothing of which He can condemn us in Jesus Christ. And so when we stand before Christ, we can have the confidence of what the Bible says in Romans 8:1—

Romans 8:1 (NIV)
"Therefore, there is now no condemnation for those who are in Christ Jesus,"

The Judgment Seat of Christ & The Marriage of the Lamb

C. At the Judgment Seat of Christ, the Motives for Our Good Works Will Be Judged.

As we have seen, our sins committed on this earth cannot be judged in Heaven at the Judgment Seat of Christ. Those outward rebellious acts toward God have already been judged when Christ died. Since this is true, why do we need a Judgment Seat of Christ at all? What is it that Christ will judge there? What will He be examining in our lives? The Bible tells us that Christ will be judging the motives or reasons for every good work we did for God.

You have often heard the phrase, "There is more to life than meets the eye." This is certainly true when it comes to our actions. For every act we carry out there is a reason for it. The Bible tells us that at the Judgment Seat of Christ, our all-knowing Judge will look beyond our good actions for God, and will reveal the motives of why we did them. Paul talks about this in 1 Corinthians 4:3-5—

> 1 Corinthians 4:3-5 (NIV)
> *3) "I care very little if I am judged by you or by any human court; indeed, I do not even judge myself.*
> *4) My conscience is clear, but that does not make me innocent. It is the Lord who judges me.*
> *5) Therefore judge nothing before the appointed time; wait till the Lord comes. He will bring to light what is hidden in darkness and will expose the motives of men's hearts. At that time each will receive his praise from God."*

The Judgment Seat of Christ & The Marriage of the Lamb

● Paul says in 1 Corinthians 4:5 that "He will bring to light... the motives of men's hearts." What do you think the word "motives" means?

_____

_____

_____

_____

The word "motives" basically means "reasons why we do what we do." We have a reason (or motive) for every action we take. These motives can be either good or bad. At the Judgment Seat of Christ, God will bring to light the reasons why we did good things for Him. And He will bring these to light because He wants to expose our real motivation and reward us for the things we did for God with pure motives.

3 | The Judgment Seat of Christ & The Marriage of the Lamb

D. At the Judgment Seat of Christ, Fire Will Test the Motives for All Our Good Works.

It is awesome to see a Christian do great things for God, whether it is preaching Christ to thousands of people or showing love and acceptance to one other person. Anything we do, big or small, that is done for God counts for eternity. But not everything that is done in the name of God is done with pure motives. Sometimes we as Christians do things for God with selfish purposes. It is often difficult to know why people do what they do for Christ. In fact, as Christians we often have a difficult time knowing what the motives are behind a good work for God. We as humans can easily be fooled. We often think that we can tell the whole book by its cover. But this is not the case. The Bible says that God looks into the heart of mankind and sees everything (Hebrews 4:13). At the Judgment Seat of Christ all of our good works will be brought forth and tested by God to see just how pure they really were. Christ will not test what we have done for God by comparing them to others or by a person's recommendation of what we have done for Him. Instead, Christ's judgment test by fire will be the only way to know whether or not what we did was truly for God. The Bible talks about this in 1 Corinthians 3:9-15—

> 1 Corinthians 3:9-15 (NIV)
> 9) "For we are God's fellow workers; you are God's field, God's building.
> 10) By the grace God has given me, I laid a foundation as an expert builder, and someone else is building on it. But each one should be careful how he builds.
> 11) For no one can lay any foundation other than the one already laid, which is Jesus Christ.
> 12) If any man builds on this foundation using gold, silver, costly stones, wood, hay, or straw,
> 13) his work will be shown for what it is, because the Day will bring it to light. It will be revealed with fire, and the fire will test the quality of each man's work.
> 14) If what he has built survives, he will receive his reward.
> 15) If it is burned up, he will suffer loss; he himself will be saved, but only as one escaping through the flames."

The Judgment Seat of Christ & The Marriage of the Lamb

- According to 1 Corinthians 3:11, what is the basis or foundation for every good thing we do for God?

_____

_____

_____

_____

Every Christian must clearly understand that anything we do that has eternal meaning must be done for Christ and by His power. Jesus Christ is the foundation for all that is good. The Bible says in Colossians 3:17—

> Colossians 3:17 (NIV)
> *"And whatever you do, whether in word or deed, do it all in the name of the Lord Jesus, giving thanks to God the Father through him."*

Anything we try to do in our own power without Christ's help will not stand at the Judgment Seat of Christ. Jesus said in John 15:5—

> John 15:5 (NIV)
> *"I am the vine; you are the branches. If a man remains in me and I in him, he will bear much fruit; apart from me you can do nothing."*

The Bible is clear that Christians build on the foundation of Jesus Christ. We cannot manufacture or counterfeit this foundation because it comes from God and God alone. We obtain this foundation when we accept Christ as our Savior. The foundation for any "good work" is Jesus Christ. And because we are building on the foundation of Christ, God is concerned with what materials we use to build. There are different types of building materials—some good, some bad. Paul talks about these different building materials in 1 Corinthians 3:12-13—

---

1 Corinthians 3:12-13 (NIV)
12) "If any man builds on this foundation using gold, silver, costly stones, wood, hay, or straw,
13) his work will be shown for what it is, because the Day will bring it to light. It will be revealed with fire, and the fire will test the quality of each man's work."

- According to 1 Corinthians 3:12, what do you think "gold, silver, and costly stones" represent?

_____

_____

_____

_____

Gold, silver, and costly stones are not only beautiful and valuable but also fireproof. They represent the actions we did for God that were done with pure motives. Anything a Christian does with pure motives that glorifies God will survive as gold.

The Judgment Seat of Christ & The Marriage of the Lamb

- According to 1 Corinthians 3:12, what do you think "wood, hay, or straw" means?

_____

_____

_____

_____

"Wood, hay, and straw" represent things we have done in God's name but were really done for ourselves. They were done with impure motives so that we might become more powerful, popular, rich or bring more glory to ourselves. They also represent anything we did for God in our own strength rather than through the power of the Holy Spirit. All of these works that are not done with the right motives, and in the power of God, will turn to ashes.

The Moment Of Truth At The Judgment Seat Of Christ

All of us will have to face that moment of truth when what we did for God will be tested by fire. It will be an exciting time for some and a time of disappointment for others.

---

1 Corinthians 3:12-15 (NIV)
12) "If any man builds on this foundation using gold, silver, costly stones, wood, hay, or straw,
13) his work will be shown for what it is, because the Day will bring it to light. It will be revealed with fire, and the fire will test the quality of each man's work.
14) If what he has built survives, he will receive his reward.
15) If it is burned up, he will suffer loss; he himself will be saved, but only as one escaping through the flames."

---

3 | The Judgment Seat of Christ & The Marriage of the Lamb

- Paul tells us that each person's work will be tested by fire. According to 1 Corinthians 3:13, what happens to the person whose good works survive the fire?

_____

_____

_____

_____

It is at this time that the good works we did for Christ with pure motives will survive the test of fire. Christ will declare these "good works" worthy of reward. It may very well be at this point that Christ will say: *"Well done, good and faithful servant!"* (Matthew 25:21). The gracious judge, Jesus Christ, will hand out the rewards. No doubt joy will flood the hearts of those who receive awards from God for what they did for Him in this life.

- According to 1 Corinthians 3:15, what will happen to those who built with "wood, hay, or straw?"

_____

_____

_____

_____

JUDGMENT SEAT OF CHRIST

2 Corinthians 5:10
"For we must all appear before the judgment seat of Christ,
that each one may receive what is due him for
the things done while in the body,
whether good or bad."

BELIEVERS'
GOOD
WORKS

GOOD WORKS
WITH PURE
MOTIVES

GOOD WORKS
DONE WITH
BAD MOTIVES

**GOOD
WORKS**

1) Gold

2) Silver

3) Precious
   Stones

REWARDS

**BAD
WORKS**

1) Wood

2) Hay

3) Straw

**LOSS of
REWARDS**

BELIEVERS' GOOD WORKS TESTED BY FIRE
1 Corinthians 3:12-15

12) "If any man builds on this foundation using gold, silver, costly stones, wood hay or straw,
13) his work will be shown for what it is, because the Day will bring it to light. It will be revealed with fire, and the fire will test the quality of each man's work.
14) If what he has built survives, he will receive his reward.
15) If it is burned up, he will suffer loss; he himself will be saved, but only as one escaping through the flames."

"Wood, hay, or straw" are inexpensive items which burn very easily. They represent the good actions we did in God's name, but were done by our own strength and for selfish reasons. The fire of Christ will quickly burn up these items showing them for what they really are—worthless. Embarrassment, shame, and perhaps heartbreak will fill the hearts of some believers as they watch much of their spiritual work turn to ashes. These Christians will not lose their salvation. Paul says that such people "will be saved, but only as one escaping through the flames." It will be something like a person who has escaped from a burning house unharmed but smelling like smoke. This person will be saved but will have a sense of loss in that they will not get a reward for their selfish work in God's name.

It should be obvious to all Christians that what we do on this earth for God is very important. We must understand that some day what we do for God will be tested at the Judgment Seat of Christ. That is why we must ask God to purify our motives and teach us to depend upon Him for everything. Or to put it another way in a popular phrase: "Only one life will soon be passed, only what's done for Christ will last." God's Word says it even more powerfully in 1 Corinthians 15:58—

---

1 Corinthians 15:58 (NIV)
"Therefore, my dear brothers, stand firm. Let nothing move you. Always give yourselves fully to the work of the Lord, because you know that your labor in the Lord is not in vain."

The Judgment Seat of Christ & The Marriage of the Lamb

II. CHRISTIANS WHOSE GOOD ACTIONS PASS THE TEST OF FIRE WILL BE REWARDED WITH INCREDIBLE CROWNS.

Christians will receive rewards in Heaven for what they have done for Christ on this earth. But what are these rewards? What kind of trophies or crowns will we receive? Are there different rewards for different Christian activities here on earth? The Bible gives us a glimpse of some of the rewards we will receive at the Judgment Seat of Christ. The rewards we will receive in Heaven, the Bible calls "crowns".

A.   What Is A Crown?

When Paul speaks of "crowns" in the New Testament, he was thinking of the crowns that were handed out at the Greek Olympic games. Each person who won his contest was given a reward. This reward was a crown of leaves from wild olive branches placed upon the heads of the victors. This crown carried a great deal of significance for the winner. It was the medal of honor, the gold medal, the blue ribbon, the first place trophy. It was the very best award a person could win as a participant in the games.[1] But these rewards were perishable. At the Judgment Seat of Christ, Christians will be given imperishable crowns for different "events" participated in here on this earth. Any Christian receiving a crown from Christ will be receiving one of the highest honors in Heaven.

---

[1] Joe Wall, *Going For The Gold,* (Chicago: Moody Press, 1991) p. 126.

B. What Crowns Will Be Given?

Though we do not have a handbook of all possible crowns listed, the Bible talks specifically about five crowns that will be awarded at the Judgment Seat of Christ. Each crown covers a particular area of the Christian life. Any Christian who is faithful in service to Christ will be rewarded with at least one of these crowns. And people could earn more than one, although very few (if any) will receive all of them. The following is a list of five crowns to be awarded.

THE FOLLOWING IS A LIST OF CROWNS THAT WILL BE GIVEN AT THE JUDGMENT SEAT OF CHRIST.

1. The Crown of Righteousness

> 2 Timothy 4:7-8 (NIV)
> *7) "I have fought the good fight, I have finished the race, I have kept the faith.*
> *8) Now there is in store for me **the crown of righteousness**, which the Lord, the righteous Judge, will award to me on that day—and not only to me, but also to all who have longed for His appearing."*

- According to 2 Timothy 4:7-8, what qualities or experiences must a Christian have to win the Crown of Righteousness?

_____

_____

_____

The Judgment Seat of Christ & 3
The Marriage of the Lamb

In order for a Christian to win the Crown of Righteousness he must be the kind of Christian who wants to please God by doing what is right. These believers may fail but their intent is to hang in there and fight to live for Christ. In order to win this wreath a Christian must also long for the Return of Jesus Christ. The Crown of Righteousness is a basic crown that God wants all Christians to win.

What About You and the Crown of Righteousness?

_____ **I feel that I am on my way to winning this Crown of Righteousness.**
DATE: _____

_____ **I make it a commitment to try to win this Crown of Righteousness.**
DATE: _____

2. The Incorruptible Crown

> 1 Corinthians 9:24-27 (NIV)
> *24) "Do you not know that in a race all the runners run, but only one gets the prize?*
> *25) Everyone who competes in the games goes into strict training. They do it to get a crown that will not last; but we do it to get a **crown that will last forever**.*
> *26) Therefore I do not run like a man running aimlessly; I do not fight like a man beating the air.*
> *27) No, I beat my body and make it my slave so that after I have preached to others, I myself will not be disqualified for the prize."*

3 | The Judgment Seat of Christ & The Marriage of the Lamb

The Judgment Seat of Christ & The Marriage of the Lamb

- According to 1 Corinthians 9:24-27, what qualities or experiences must a Christian have in order to win the Incorruptible Crown?

_____

_____

_____

_____

The Incorruptible Crown is a more difficult crown to win. This crown goes to the Christian who is willing to be like a top athlete or a Marine. That is to say, this person is willing to go into strict training. In the apostle Paul's day, even though a participant may win an Olympic race, if he broke the rules while in training, he would forfeit the crown. A Christian who wins the Incorruptible Crown is one who is willing to deny himself and many of his personal desires in order to live for Christ. This Christian doesn't just try to stay away from sin. But, because of his priorities he will even turn away from some of the "good" activities that other Christians enjoy.

What About You and the Incorruptible Crown?

_____ **I feel that I am on my way to winning this Incorruptible Crown.**
DATE: _____

_____ **I make it a commitment to try to win this Incorruptible Crown.**
DATE: _____

3. The Crown of Life

> James 1:12 (NIV)
> *"Blessed is the man who perseveres under trial, because when he has stood the test, he will receive the **crown of life** that God has promised to those who love him."*
>
> Revelation 2:10 (NIV)
> *"Do not be afraid of what you are about to suffer. I tell you, the Devil will put some of you in prison to test you, and you will suffer persecution for ten days. Be faithful, even to the point of death, and I will give you the **crown of life.**"*

• According to James 1:12 and Revelation 2:10, what qualities or experiences must a Christian have in order to win the Crown of Life?

_____

_____

_____

_____

The Crown of Life will be awarded to those who have served God under intense suffering and persecution. In fact, this crown is often called the "Martyrs Crown" because it will be rewarded to those who suffered great persecution and even martyrdom for the sake of Christ.

What About You and the Crown of Life?

_____ I feel that I am on my way to winning this Crown of Life.
DATE: _____

_____ I make it a commitment to try to win this Crown of Life.
DATE: _____

The Judgment Seat of Christ & The Marriage of the Lamb

4. The Crown of Joy

1 Thessalonians 2:19-20 (NIV)
*19) "For what is our hope, **our joy, or the crown** in which we will glory in the presence of our Lord Jesus when he comes? Is it not you?*
*20) Indeed, you are **our glory and joy.**"*

Philippians 4:1 (NIV)
*"Therefore, my brothers, you whom I love and long for, **my joy and crown,** that is how you should stand firm in the Lord, dear friends!"*

● According to 1 Thessalonians 2:19-20 and Philippians 4:1, what qualities or experiences must a Christian have in order to win the Crown of Joy?

_____

_____

_____

_____

The Crown of Joy will be awarded to those who, for the sake of Jesus, have poured their lives into others. This crown is sometimes called the "Soul-winners Crown." It will be given to those who have made it their life's ambition to lead others to Christ and help them grow as Christians.

The Judgment Seat of Christ & The Marriage of the Lamb

What About You and the Crown of Joy?

_____ I feel that I am on my way to winning this Crown of Joy.
DATE: _____

_____ I make it a commitment to try to win this Crown of Joy.
DATE: _____

5. The Crown of Glory

> 1 Peter 5:1, 4 (NIV)
> *1) "To the elders among you, I appeal as a fellow elder, a witness of Christ's sufferings and one who also will share in the glory to be revealed...*
> *4) And when the Chief Shepherd appears, you will receive the **crown of glory** that will never fade away."*

- According to 1 Peter 5:1, 4, what qualities or experiences must a Christian have in order to win the Crown of Glory?

_____

_____

_____

_____

The Crown of Glory is a special crown for those who teach Christ's Word. It is sometimes called the "Elder's Crown." People who will earn an "Elder's Crown" could be ministers, deacons and elders, Sunday school teachers, youth pastors etc. It is a big responsibility and hard work to be able to teach God's Word and help other people to live it. God will reward those who have been faithful to teach His Word with a Crown of Glory.

The Judgment Seat of Christ & The Marriage of the Lamb

What About You And the Crown of Glory?

_____ **I feel that I am on my way to winning this Crown of Glory.**
DATE: _____

_____ **I make it a commitment to try to win this Crown of Glory.**
DATE: _____

What a time for believers the Judgment Seat of Christ will be! It will be a time of awe and joy as we receive these incredible crowns and trophies that will last forever. But the Bible tells us that we will be so moved by Christ Himself at this time that we will lay our crowns down at His feet (Revelation 4:10). We also will be blown away when Christ gives us new responsibilities for future service to Him for Eternity. On that day, all those who receive a reward will be thrilled that while on this earth they did something that counted for Eternity. Therefore every Christian should remember the promise of Jesus Christ found in Revelation 22:12-13—

Revelation 22:12-13 (NIV)
12) "Behold, I am coming soon! My reward is with me, and I will give to everyone according to what he has done.
13) I am the Alpha and the Omega, the First and the Last, the Beginning and the End."

The Judgment Seat of Christ & 3 The Marriage of the Lamb

III. IT IS VERY IMPORTANT THAT WE CLEARLY UNDERSTAND THE BEAUTIFUL EVENT THAT WILL TAKE PLACE IN HEAVEN CALLED THE WEDDING OF THE LAMB.

It is amazing to consider all that Jesus Christ has gone through to love us and work in us so that we might be with Him in Heaven forever! He has done this because He has chosen to love us and wants to be close to us. So close is the tie that Jesus wants with us, that in the Bible Christ is called a Husband. Those who believe in Him are called His Bride. The apostle Paul in 2 Corinthians 11 and Ephesians 5 talked about this incredible relationship that Jesus has planned for us—

2 Corinthians 11:2 (NIV)
"I am jealous for you with a godly jealousy. I promised you to one husband, to Christ, so that I might present you as a pure virgin to him."

Ephesians 5:25-27; 32 (NIV)
25) "Husbands, love your wives, just as Christ loved the church and gave Himself up for her.
26) to make her holy, cleansing her by the washing with water through the word,
27) and to present her to Himself as a radiant church, without stain or wrinkle or any other blemish, but holy and blameless....
32) This is a profound mystery—but I am talking about Christ and the church."

3 | The Judgment Seat of Christ & The Marriage of the Lamb

• In 2 Corinthians 11:2, what is Christ called?

_____

_____

_____

_____

• According to 2 Corinthians 11:2, what are Believers in Christ called?

_____

_____

_____

_____

• Why do you think the Bible uses the example of a Bridegroom and a Bride to talk about His relationship to Christians?

_____

_____

_____

_____

The Judgment Seat of Christ & The Marriage of the Lamb

● According to Ephesians 5:26-27, what does Christ want to do for His bride?

_____

_____

_____

_____

Jesus is working to cleanse those who believe in Him (the Bride) so that one day we will be presented to Him as a spiritually pure, beautiful and radiant bride. This has been Christ's eternal goal for us. The Bible tells us that we belong to Christ the moment we trust Him as our Savior. Yet in Heaven, after the Judgment Seat of Christ, there will be a formal and beautiful moment when we will stand pure before Christ and a wedding will take place. The Bible talks about this beautiful moment in Revelation 19:7-8—

> Revelation 19:7-8 (NIV)
> 7) *"Let us rejoice and be glad and give Him glory! For the wedding of the Lamb has come, and His bride has made herself ready.*
> 8) *Fine linen, bright and clean, was given her to wear. (Fine linen stands for the righteous acts of the saints.)"*

**The Judgment Seat of Christ &
The Marriage of the Lamb**

● According to Revelation 19:7, how will we all feel at this great Wedding Ceremony?

_____

_____

_____

_____

This beautiful wedding ceremony between Jesus and us will give us joy like we have never known before. We will be in awe of the brilliance of Jesus Christ and be overwhelmed that we are so close to Him.

● According to Revelation 19:8, what will we be wearing at the Great Wedding in Heaven?

_____

_____

_____

_____

● What does the beautiful clothing that we will be wearing stand for?

_____

_____

_____

The Judgment Seat of Christ & The Marriage of the Lamb

Never will we be better dressed than at the wedding of Christ. Somehow all the righteous acts for which we were rewarded at the Judgment Seat of Christ will cover our resurrection bodies in brilliant beauty.

There never has nor will there ever be another wedding like this! On that day, we will all be thrilled beyond our wildest imaginations that we are with Jesus and Jesus is with us. We also will be amazed at our own beauty: a beauty which will be a reflection of Christ. The Bible talks about this beauty in Daniel 12:3—

> Daniel 12:3 (NIV)
> *"Those who are wise will shine like the brightness of the heavens, and those who lead many to righteousness, like the stars for ever and ever."*

IN CONCLUSION

A day is coming when we will stand before Christ. On that day, as we are prepared for our rewards and the great wedding ceremony in Heaven, our good works will be judged. What we do today will greatly affect what will happen on that day. It would be wise for us to live in the light of that Day. As surely as we are alive now, that great Day will come. As believers, Jesus wants preparing for heaven to be the greatest priority in our lives. The Bible says in Matthew 6:19-21—

> Matthew 6:19-21 (NIV)
> *19) "Do not store up for yourselves treasures on earth, where moth and rust destroy, and where thieves break in and steal.*
> *20) But store up for yourselves treasures in Heaven, where moth and rust do not destroy, and where thieves do not break in and steal.*
> *21) For where your treasure is, there your heart will be also."*

4 | The Second Coming of Christ & The Millennium

4 The Second Coming of Christ & The Millennium

As we saw in the last chapter, some amazing things will be taking place in Heaven after the Rapture. Those living after Christ's Resurrection who have believed in Him (the Church), will be in Heaven. At that time they will be involved in the Judgment Seat of Christ and celebrating the Marriage of the Lamb. Meanwhile back on earth incredible events will be taking place. After the Rapture, the world will go into intense suffering in a period called the Tribulation. The Tribulation is a seven year period that will take place before the Second Coming of Jesus Christ. It will be a time when Satan reigns through the Antichrist, when men show their absolute rebellion towards God, and God pours out His judgments on mankind. At the end of the Tribulation, life will be unbearable. The Antichrist and his False Prophet will have moved into world control. (See chapter six of *Pack Your Bags - Jesus is Coming!* a discussion manual by Dawson McAllister which teaches about the return of Christ and the Great Tribulation.) With the Antichrist's ruthless rule, he will seem destined to be the world's dictator for years to come. Yet God is the one who ultimately is in charge of the world. God is the one who sets the times of history. While it will appear that the Antichrist is in charge, God will quickly bring history as we know it to a close.

The Bible tells us that God will dramatically step into time with one of the greatest events in eternal history. After the Tribulation, during the great Battle of Armageddon, Jesus will Return to this earth. He will return to destroy the work of Satan and to rule on this earth for a thousand years.

IN THIS CHAPTER WE WILL DISCUSS WHAT WILL HAPPEN AT THE SECOND COMING OF CHRIST, AND HIS THOUSAND YEAR REIGN, KNOWN AS THE MILLENNIUM.

---

4 | The Second Coming of Christ & The Millennium

The Second Coming of Christ & The Millennium

4

I. AT THE SECOND COMING, JESUS CHRIST WILL RETURN AS A MIGHTY WARRIOR TO DEFEAT HIS ENEMIES.

A. Jesus Christ Will Return as a Mighty Warrior

History will never be the same again once Jesus comes back to judge the world at His Second Coming. He will come in such an incredibly powerful way that all will know that He has come to set up a whole new kind of living on this earth. When Jesus Christ comes back to judge and to change this world it will be in a very dramatic way. The Bible talks about Christ's Second Coming in Matthew 24:27; 29-30—

Matthew 24:27; 29-30 (NKJV)

27) "For as the lightning comes from the east and flashes to the west, so also will the coming of the Son of Man be.

29) Immediately after the tribulation of those days the sun will be darkened, and the moon will not give its light; the stars will fall from heaven, and the powers of the heavens will be shaken.

30) Then the sign of the Son of Man will appear in heaven, and then all the tribes of the earth will mourn, and they will see the Son of Man coming on the clouds of heaven with power and great glory."

• According to Matthew 24:27; 29-30, how do we know that the coming of Jesus Christ will be very dramatic?

---

4 The Second Coming of Christ & The Millennium

What a moment that will be. The world will become totally dark. Stars will fall from Heaven. His brilliant glory will flash across the sky like lightning.

- According to Matthew 24:30, how will people respond to Christ's Return?

_____

_____

_____

_____

- Why will the people who are on the earth at the moment of Christ's Return mourn?

_____

_____

_____

_____

Most of the people on the earth at the moment of Christ's Return will be in rebellion against God. Yet, they will look up and see the one they hate so much—Jesus—coming in great power and brilliance. The Bible tells us in Revelation 19:14 that Christ will come with the "armies of heaven." These armies of heaven will be Christians who are now ready to return with Christ and rule with Him for a thousand years. The world will begin to understand that Jesus Christ has come back to judge the world and to rule forever. They will mourn because they will realize they have been defeated by Jesus Christ. In just a short time the world's armies will be defeated and crushed by Christ at His Second Coming.

The Second Coming of Christ & The Millennium

B.   Jesus Christ Will Return to this Earth to Defeat the Armies of the World.

People will mourn when they see Christ coming because they will quickly know that their enemy Jesus Christ has come back with incredible power. The armies of the World will have already been gathered together for the great battle of Armageddon. The Bible tells us that they will turn from fighting each other to fight against Christ and His armies. John saw a vision about what would take place when Christ encountered the armies of the world. Revelation 19:11-18 tells us—

Revelation 19:11-18 (NIV)

11) "I saw heaven standing open and there before me was a white horse, whose rider is called Faithful and True. With justice he judges and makes war.

12) His eyes are like blazing fire, and on his head are many crowns. He has a name written on him that no one knows but He Himself.

13) He is dressed in a robe dipped in blood, and his name is the Word of God.

14) The armies of heaven were following him, riding on white horses and dressed in fine linen, white and clean.

15) Out of his mouth comes a sharp sword with which to strike down the nations. 'He will rule them with an iron scepter.' He treads the winepress of the fury of the wrath of God Almighty.

16) On his robe and on his thigh he has this name written: KING OF KINGS AND LORD OF LORDS.

17) And I saw an angel standing in the sun, who cried in a loud voice to all the birds flying in midair, 'Come, gather together for the great supper of God,

18) so that you may eat the flesh of kings, generals, and mighty men, of horses and their riders, and the flesh of all people, free and slave, small and great.'"

---

4 The Second Coming of Christ & The Millennium

The Second Coming of Christ & The Millennium

● According to Revelation 19:11-16, how is Christ described?

_____

_____

_____

_____

There has never before been anyone like Christ when He comes to this earth to make war. He will come with eyes like blazing fire, riding a white horse. There will be many crowns on His head and He will be wearing a special robe. Tens of millions of Christians will be following Him riding white horses as well. He will have a sharp sword (or maybe just the word of His mouth) with which He will strike down and devastate the armies of the world.

● According to Revelation 19:17-18, how do we know the armies of the world suffer great defeat?

_____

_____

_____

_____

According to Revelation 19:17-18, people of every walk of life will meet their doom at the hands of Jesus. The angels witnessed this great war and called the birds of the air to come and eat the flesh of all people. The great armies of the world will have no chance against the mighty warrior Jesus Christ.

C. Jesus Christ Will Return to this Earth to Defeat the Antichrist & False Prophet.

Christ will come not only to defeat the nations of the world but also to defeat the fierce Antichrist and His False Prophet. The Bible tells us that the Antichrist will be the most evil and godless man who will ever live. Empowered by Satan himself, the Antichrist will use any means possible to set himself up as god. He will desperately long for the worship of the world. And to help achieve his goal of worldwide worship, the Antichrist will have the assistance of the False Prophet. The False Prophet will have incredible powers to deceive the masses. He will use all of this power to exalt the Antichrist. The Antichrist and False Prophet force all those who will worship him to wear the 'mark of the beast' which is the number 666. The Antichrist and his False Prophet will hate Christ but will be powerless to stop Him at His coming. They will be completely defeated. John talked about this great defeat of the Antichrist and the False Prophet in Revelation 19:19-21—

Revelation 19:19-21 (NIV)
19) "Then I saw the beast and the kings of the earth and their armies gathered together to make war against the rider on the horse and his army.
20) But the beast was captured, and with him the false prophet who had performed the miraculous signs on his behalf. With these signs he had deluded those who had received the mark of the beast and worshipped his image. The two of them were thrown alive into the fiery lake of burning sulfur.
21) The rest of them were killed with the sword that came out of the mouth of the rider on the horse, and all the birds gorged themselves on their flesh."

The Second Coming of Christ & The Millennium

● According to Revelation 19:19-21, what two things happen to the Beast and the False Prophet when Christ Returns?

_____

_____

_____

_____

Christ will come with such brilliant power that the Antichrist and the False Prophet will be destroyed by the splendor of His Coming (2 Thessalonians 2:8). As we have seen in Scripture the Antichrist and the False Prophet will be thrown into the 'Lake of Fire.' In a sense, these two will become the first prisoners of Hell.

4 | The Second Coming of Christ & The Millennium

The Second Coming of Christ & The Millennium

D. **Jesus Christ Will Return to this Earth and Satan Will Be Locked Away for a Thousand Years.**

Satan is the source of all sin and lies. For centuries he has waged war against God. But at the Second Coming of Jesus Christ, God will render Satan useless and lock him away for a thousand years. The apostle John saw a vision of this taking place and told us about it in Revelation 20:1-3—

Revelation 20:1-3 (NIV)
1) "And I saw an angel coming down out of heaven, having the key to the Abyss and holding in his hand a great chain.
2) He seized the dragon, that ancient serpent, who is the devil, or Satan, and bound him for a thousand years.
3) He threw him into the Abyss, and locked and sealed it over him, to keep him from deceiving the nations anymore until the thousand years were ended. After that, he must be set free for a short time."

● According to Revelation 20:1-3, Satan is locked and sealed in what the Bible calls the 'Abyss.' What do you think the Abyss is?

_____

_____

_____

_____

The 'Abyss' is the Biblical name for the headquarters of Satan and his demons. Most likely, not only Satan, but all of his demons will be locked in there as well. This will be God's version of a 'house arrest.'

- According to Revelation 20:1-3, why will Satan be locked up in the 'Abyss?'

_____

_____

_____

_____

Satan's lies have all but destroyed mankind. If it wasn't for God's goodness his deceiving ways would have lead everyone to ruin. The Bible says that for a thousand years he will be locked up and will be unable to fool anyone.

E. When Jesus Christ Returns to this Earth He Will Judge Those Who Are Still Living at His Return.

The Antichrist will not have killed everyone who believed in Christ during the Tribulation. There will be some new Christians who are still alive when Jesus Christ Returns. At the same time not every unbeliever will be killed at the Second Coming of Christ. There will be those who will survive that climatic event. What will happen to these people? Jesus taught His disciples that on that Day He would judge everyone who was still living and separate the good from the bad. Jesus talks about this in Matthew 25:31-46—

The Second Coming of Christ & The Millennium

Christ Separates The Sheep From the Goats

Matthew 25:31-46 (NIV)

31) "When the Son of Man comes in His glory, and all the angels with Him, He will sit on His throne in heavenly glory.

32) All the nations will be gathered before Him, and He will separate the people one from another as a shepherd separates the sheep from the goats.

33) He will put the sheep on His right and the goats on His left.

34) Then the King will say to those on His right, 'Come, you who are blessed by my Father; take your inheritance, the kingdom prepared for you since the creation of the world.

35) For I was hungry and you gave me something to eat, I was thirsty and you gave me something to drink, I was a stranger and you invited me in,

36) I needed clothes and you clothed me, I was sick and you looked after me, I was in prison and you came to visit me.'

37) Then the righteous will answer Him, 'Lord, when did we see you hungry and feed you, or thirsty and give you something to drink?

38) When did we see you a stranger and invite you in, or needing clothes and clothe you?

39) When did we see you sick or in prison and go to visit you?'

40) The King will reply, 'I tell you the truth, whatever you did for one of the least of these brothers of mine, you did for me.'

41) Then He will say to those on His left, 'Depart from me, you who are cursed, into the eternal fire prepared for the devil and his angels.

42) For I was hungry and you gave me nothing to eat, I was thirsty and you gave me nothing to drink,

43) I was a stranger and you did not invite me in, I needed clothes and you did not clothe me, I was sick and in prison and you did not look after me.'

44) They also will answer, 'Lord, when did we see you hungry or thirsty or a stranger or needing clothes or sick or in prison, and did not help you?

45) He will reply, 'I tell you the truth, whatever you did not do for one of the least of these, you did not do for me.'

46) Then they will go away to eternal punishment, but the righteous to eternal life."

4 | The Second Coming of Christ & The Millennium

• According to Matthew 25:32, Jesus will separate the people still living at His Return into two groups. What are they?

_____

_____

_____

_____

Those who survive the Second Coming of Christ will all be gathered before Christ. At that time Christ will separate people into groups of sheep and goats.

• According to Matthew 25:33-40, how does Christ describe those who are 'sheep?'

_____

_____

_____

_____

During the Tribulation, life will be horrible for those who do not believe in the Antichrist. It will be a time when Christians (especially Jewish believers) will be persecuted beyond belief. Anyone who would risk helping a Christian would be putting his or her life in danger. No one would risk helping a Christian unless that person was a Christian himself. And so Christ describes 'sheep' as those who did good things for Believers. Because in doing good things for Believers they were doing them out of a love for Christ. And their reward is that they will enter into Christ's kingdom as living individuals who have not been resurrected. These individuals will populate the Millennium.

The Second Coming of Christ & The Millennium

● According to Matthew 25:41-46, how does Christ describe those who are 'goats?'

_____

_____

_____

_____

During the Tribulation most people will reject Christ and follow the Antichrist. They will be deceived by him and will obey his commands. To offer help to someone who did not have the mark of the beast would be high treason. The followers of the Antichrist will hate Christians and persecute them. Christ will judge them guilty of rejecting Him and will sentence them to the 'lake of fire.'

F. When Christ Returns Many People Will Rise from the Dead.

When Christ Returns it will be a time of tremendous spiritual and physical activity. It will be a time when God in a powerful way will supernaturally invade this world. And when Christ's tremendous power is unleashed at the Second Coming, a truly amazing thing will happen. People will rise from the dead. But who are these people that will rise from the dead? John tells us who these dead people are in Revelation 20:4-6—

Revelation 20:4-6 (NIV)

4) "I saw thrones on which were seated those who had been given authority to judge. And I saw the souls of those who had been beheaded because of their testimony for Jesus and because of the word of God. They had not worshipped the beast or his image and had not received his mark on their foreheads or their hands. They came to life and reigned with Christ a thousand years.

5) [The rest of the dead did not come to life until the thousand years were ended.] This is the first resurrection.

6) Blessed and holy are those who have part in the first resurrection. The second death has no power over them, but they will be priests of God and of Christ and will reign with him for a thousand years."

● According to Revelation 20:4-6, who are these people who rise from the dead?

_____

_____

_____

_____

Because of God's incredible work through His angels, the Two Witnesses, and the 144,000 Jewish evangelists, many people will come to Christ during the Tribulation. The Antichrist's intense desire to be worshipped as god will drive him to kill anyone who does not bow down to him. He will kill tens of thousands of believers during this time. John tells us that these believers will be resurrected at the Second Coming of Christ to reign with Him for a thousand years.

The Second Coming of Christ & 4
The Millennium

Not only will these Tribulation believers be resurrected, but also those Old Testament believers such as Moses, David, Solomon, Isaiah, Daniel etc. will be as well. Daniel speaks of this resurrection in Daniel 12:1-2—

Daniel 12:1-2 (NIV)
1) "At that time Michael, the great prince who protects your people, will arise. There will be a time of distress such as has not happened from the beginning of nations until then. But at that time your people—everyone whose name is found written in the book—will be delivered.
2) Multitudes who sleep in the dust of the earth will awake: some to everlasting life, others to shame and everlasting contempt."

When Christ returns He will come as a mighty Warrior. He will show Himself as what He is—God who is ready to judge the world for her rebellion. No one will be able to stand against His mighty power. Nations of the world will be destroyed. The Antichrist and his False Prophet will be thrown into Hell. And Satan himself will be locked away for a thousand years. It will be an awful time for those who refused to follow Jesus Christ but a great day for those who love Him.

Jesus Himself tells us in Matthew 24:35 that all He has promised will come to pass—

Matthew 24:35 (NIV)
"Heaven and earth will pass away, but my words will never pass away."

4 | The Second Coming of Christ & The Millennium

HEAVEN

JUDGMENT SEAT OF CHRIST
We will stand before Christ and He will judge all our "good works" for Him. Those with pure motives will be rewarded.

MARRIAGE SUPPER OF THE LAMB
We will be presented to Christ as spiritually pure and perfect.

SECOND COMING
Christ will come back to earth with His followers.

- Christ will defeat the armies of the world.

- Christ will defeat the Antichrist and False Prophet.

- Satan will be locked away for a 1,000 years.

- Christ will judge those who are still alive at His coming.

- Christians who died during the Tribulation will rise from the dead.

RAPTURE
Christ will come _for_ His followers.

ANY MOMENT NOW

EARTH

◄TRIBULATION►
A 7-year period of intense suffering following the rapture.

MILLENNIUM
The 1,000-year reign of Christ on earth.

The Second Coming of Christ & The Millennium | 4

II. AFTER THE SECOND COMING, JESUS CHRIST WILL SET UP HIS KINGDOM ON EARTH AND REIGN FOR A THOUSAND YEARS.

In Revelation 20, the apostle John had an incredible vision of what would happen after the Return of Christ. He saw Satan being locked away for a thousand years (Revelation 20:1-3). He then saw the believers who had been killed during the Tribulation, be resurrected from the dead. John said of these people in Revelation 20:4d-6—

> Revelation 20:4d-6 (NIV)
> 4) *"…They came to life and reigned with Christ a thousand years.*
> 5) *[The rest of the dead did not come to life until the thousand years were ended.] This is the first resurrection.*
> 6) *Blessed and holy are those who have part in the first resurrection. The second death has no power over them, but they will be priests of God and of Christ and will reign with him for a thousand years."*

In this amazing vision John spoke of the reign of Christ after His Second Coming. This thousand-year reign of Christ on earth is known as the Millennium.

What is the Millennium?

The word "Millennium" is Latin for a thousand years. It refers to a future time after the Second Coming of Christ. The Millennium will be a thousand-year period when Christ will rule on this earth bringing justice and peace to all mankind. This great Millennium was spoken of by the Prophets in the Old Testament, and will be truly amazing. During this time Christ will bring purity to a world that for so long has been wicked. He will bring peace to a world that has been torn apart by the destruction of war. He will bring prosperity to a world that has been economically destroyed. At long last, God will show what a wonderful world it can be when everything is under Christ's control. It will be an incredible time to be alive.

4 | The Second Coming of Christ & The Millennium

The Second Coming of Christ & The Millennium | 4

A.   During the Millennium, Christ Will Rule from Jerusalem and Bring to the World, Peace, Justice, and Righteousness.

The world has always longed for Peace but has never been able to find it. In the hearts of every person is a sense of fairness and justice. But for all of our longing for Justice, precious little is found. However, the Bible says that one day all the things that a weary world has longed for will come about when Jesus will rule from Jerusalem. The great Old Testament prophet Isaiah spoke of the great reign of Christ from this city when he prophesied in Isaiah 2:2-4—

Isaiah 2:2-4 (NIV)

2) "In the last days the mountain of the Lord's temple will be established as chief among the mountains; it will be raised above the hills, and all nations will stream to it.

3) Many peoples will come and say, 'Come, let us go up to the mountain of the Lord, to the house of the God of Jacob. He will teach us his ways, so that we may walk in his paths.' The law will go out from Zion, the word of the Lord from Jerusalem.

4) He will judge between the nations and will settle disputes for many peoples. They will beat their swords into plowshares and their spears into pruning hooks. Nation will not take up sword against nation, nor will they train for war anymore."

---

4 | The Second Coming of Christ & The Millennium

- In Isaiah 2:2, the prophet tells us that the Lord's Temple will be extremely important. According to the Scripture how do we know this is true?

_____

_____

_____

_____

- According to Isaiah 2:3, how do we know that Christ will rule from Jerusalem?

_____

_____

_____

_____

God has always loved the city of Jerusalem. It is from there that He ruled through His kings and spoke through His prophets about His plans for Eternity. It was in Jerusalem that God had built the Holy Temple where the children of Israel offered sacrifices to Him. It was in Jerusalem that Christ was sentenced to death and crucified. And it will be in Jerusalem that Christ will set up His kingdom to rule this earth for a thousand years.

The Second Coming of Christ & The Millennium

- According to Isaiah 2:4, how do we know that there will be peace during the Millennium?

_____

_____

_____

_____

The most precious commodity in all the world is peace. But peace has been almost impossible to find. When peoples and nations have disputes they will often turn to violence to attempt settlements. But during the thousand-year reign of Christ there will be no wars or violence because the greatest Judge in all Eternity, Jesus Christ, will settle disputes between nations. Not one bit of money or time will be used for the training or fighting of wars. Jesus Christ will be the King and whatever He says or does will be perfect. When predicting the birth of Jesus Christ, Isaiah also prophesied that one day Christ will lead the greatest government of all time. He spoke of this in Isaiah 9:6-7—

Isaiah 9:6-7 (NIV)
6) "For to us a child is born, to us a son is given, and the government will be on His shoulders. And He will be called Wonderful Counselor, Mighty God, Everlasting Father, Prince of Peace.
7) Of the increase of His government and peace there will be no end. He will reign on David's throne and over His kingdom, establishing and upholding it with justice and righteousness from that time on and forever. The zeal of the Lord Almighty will accomplish this."

The Second Coming of Christ & The Millennium

B. During the Millennium, the Presence of God Will Be Felt Everywhere.

Most Christians have had moving experiences with God at one time or another. Perhaps this great moment with God happened at a camp or some kind of meeting where intense teaching and praise was taking place. Or perhaps it was during an all-night prayer meeting that God's presence seemed so real. It can be incredibly exciting for Christians to be around each other experiencing the presence of God. During the Millennium the closeness of Christ and the thrill of being with other Christians will be felt worldwide. Since Christ will be on this earth and most every person living at that time will be believing in Jesus, it will be an incredibly powerful time. Jeremiah spoke of the worldwide influence in Jeremiah 31:33b-34—

> Jeremiah 31:33b-34 (NIV)
> 33) *"...I will put my law in their minds and write it on their hearts. I will be their God, and they will be my people.*
> 34) *No longer will a man teach his neighbor, or a man his brother, saying, 'Know the Lord,' because they will all know me, from the least of them to the greatest, declares the Lord. 'For I will forgive their wickedness and will remember their sins no more."*

● According to Jeremiah 31:33, what two things will God do with His law?

_____

_____

_____

_____

● According to Jeremiah 31:34, will there be anybody who does not know about the Lord?

_____

_____

_____

_____

The Millennium will be a time when God will write His law in the minds and hearts of all those who enter into this kingdom. The spiritual presence of God will be so powerful that a man will no longer approach a neighbor or friend who does not know about God. The prophet Isaiah wrote of how widespread the knowledge of God will be—

Isaiah 11:9 (NIV)
"They will neither harm nor destroy on all my holy mountain,
for the earth will be full of the knowledge of the Lord as the waters
cover the sea."

The widespread knowledge of God, as well as Christ's physical presence, will set the stage for an amazing spiritual life during the Millennium. In a way like never before, the Holy Spirit will have an awesome and powerful influence in the lives of believers throughout the Millennium. The prophet Joel tells us of this mighty outpouring of God's Holy Spirit in Joel 2:28-29—

The Second Coming of Christ & The Millennium

> Joel 2:28-29 (NIV)
> *28) "And afterward, I will pour out my Spirit on all people. Your sons and daughters will prophesy, your old men will dream dreams, your young men will see visions.*
> *29) Even on my servants, both men and women, I will pour out my Spirit in those days."*

During the Millennium there will be no opposition from Satan or His demonic world. The Holy Spirit will move among the peoples of the world in an incredible and powerful way. There will be love, joy, and peace on this earth like never seen before in the history of the world.

C. During the Millennium, Man Will Experience Wealth and Health.

Life in the Millennium will basically be the way God had originally planned it to be. Christ will rule from Jerusalem. People will live in peace and enjoy the presence of God like never before. The negative stresses of everyday living will be diminished and man will enjoy life to its fullest. For the first time since the fall of man, poverty will be destroyed and the whole world will prosper. The prophet Amos predicted how awesome this time of prosperity will be. He said in Amos 9:13—

> Amos 9:13 (NIV)
> *"The days are coming", declares the Lord, "when the reaper will be overtaken by the plowman and the planter by the one treading grapes. New wine will drip from the mountains and flow from all the hills."*

The Second Coming of Christ & The Millennium

• What do you think Amos meant when he said, "The days are coming when the reaper will be overtaken by the plowman?"

_____

_____

_____

_____

Those living during the time of the Millennium will not be able to keep up with the abundance of blessings that God will give them. No one will go to bed worrying about paying their bills or where their next meal will come from. Every person alive will be secure in the love and blessings of God.

The Second Coming of Christ & The Millennium

During the Millennial, Hospitals will not be Needed

One fear that every person has today is the fear of getting sick and not being able to live a healthy life. All around us we see people suffering from various kinds of physical affliction. Almost everyone lives with the fear of an untimely death, or of not being able to experience all that life has to offer. But in the Millennium, no one will have those fears. The prophet Isaiah tells of the health and long life of those who will live in the Millennium.

Isaiah 33:24 (NIV)
"No one living in Zion will say, 'I am ill"; and the sins of those who dwell there will be forgiven."

Isaiah 35:5-6 (NIV)
5) "Then will the eyes of the blind be opened and the ears of the deaf unstopped.
6) Then will the lame leap like a deer, and the mute tongue shout for joy. Water will gush forth in the wilderness and streams in the desert."

Isaiah 65:20 (NIV)
"Never again will there be in it an infant who lives but a few days, or an old man who does not live out his years; he who dies at a hundred will be thought a mere youth; he who fails to reach a hundred will be considered accursed."

4 | The Second Coming of Christ & The Millennium

The Second Coming of Christ & The Millennium

• According to Isaiah 33:24, will anyone be discussing their physical illnesses during the thousand-year reign of Christ?

_____

_____

_____

_____

• According to Isaiah 35:5-6, what will happen to those who have physical ailments as they enter the Millennium?

_____

_____

_____

_____

• According to Isaiah 65:20, how old do you think people might be when they die?

_____

_____

_____

_____

The Second Coming of Christ & The Millennium

No one knows for sure just how long people will live during the great thousand year reign of Christ. There are those who say that people will die during the Millennium. Others say 'no;' those living at that time will live the full thousand years. Either way, at the time of the thousand-year reign of Christ people will live a long and healthy life—longer than anyone could fathom in this world.

IN CONCLUSION

At the worst possible time in history, at the end of the Tribulation, Christ will Return. He will come to destroy the work of Satan and the rebellious armies of the world. Satan will be locked away for a thousand years. Christ will judge those who are still living at His Return. Then He will usher in a thousand years of love, joy, peace, prosperity, and health. And those who know Christ will reign with Him for a thousand years. It will be a time like earth experienced before the fall of man. Notice what the prophet Isaiah has to say in Isaiah 11:6-8—

Isaiah 11:6-8 (NIV)
6) "The wolf will live with the lamb, the leopard will lie down with the goat, the calf and the lion and the yearling together; and a little child will lead them.
7) The cow will feed with the bear, their young will lie down together, and the lion will eat straw like the ox.
8) The infant will play near the hole of the cobra, and the young child put his hand into the viper's nest."

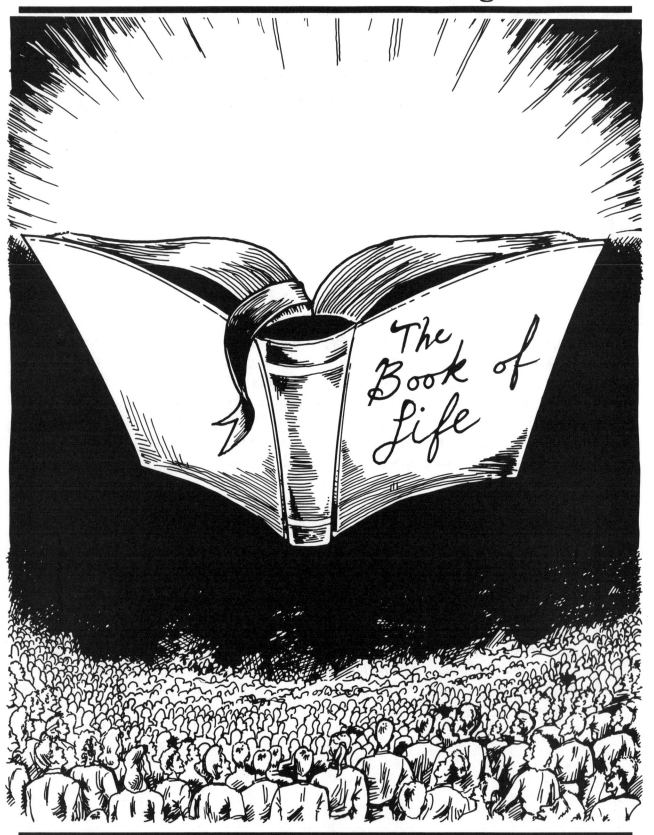

5 | Satan's Final Rebellion & The Great White Throne Judgment

The previous chapter demonstrated that the thousand-year reign of Christ, the Millennium, will be incredible. For a thousand years Jesus Christ will reign on this earth and bring peace, justice, and prosperity to the world. The Bible tells us that during the Millennium people will live much longer than ever and have a life full of health and wealth. Yet in spite of the knowledge of God and His love going throughout the world, there will still be a major rebellion at the end of the thousand years of Christ's earthly reign. The thousand year reign of Christ will end in a great battle. In that battle, Christ will shatter Satan and the awfulness of sin forever. He will then bring judgment against everyone that has refused to trust Him as Savior.

> **IN THIS CHAPTER WE WILL DISCUSS SATAN AND MANKIND'S FINAL REBELLION AGAINST GOD AND CHRIST'S FINAL JUDGMENT AT THE GREAT WHITE THRONE ON ALL OF THOSE WHO HAVE REJECTED HIM.**

5 | Satan's Final Rebellion & The Great White Throne Judgment

I. SATAN WILL ORCHESTRATE MANKIND'S FINAL REBELLION AGAINST GOD.

At the close of the Millennium an awful sequence of events will be started. The apostle John saw a vision of this tragic series of events in Revelation 20:7-10—

> Revelation 20:7-10 (NIV)
> 7) *"When the thousand years are over, Satan will be released from his prison*
> 8) *and will go out to deceive the nations in the four corners of the earth—Gog and Magog—to gather them for battle. In number they are like the sand on the seashore.*
> 9) *They marched across the breadth of the earth and surrounded the camp of God's people, the city he loves. But fire came down from heaven and devoured them.*
> 10) *And the devil, who deceived them, was thrown into the lake of burning sulfur, where the beast and the false prophet had been thrown. They will be tormented day and night for ever and ever."*

A. Satan Will Be Released from the Abyss

The Millennium will be a time of prosperity never before seen in the history of the world. There will be no war, famine, or sickness to destroy those living at that time. By the time the thousand-year reign of Christ is over, tens of millions of people will have filled the earth and will know of Christ's love, wisdom, and power. But after the thousand years are over something amazing will take place. John had a vision in Revelation 20:7 of what will happen to Satan at the end of reign of Christ—

> Revelation 20:7 (NIV)
> *"When the thousand years are over, Satan will be released from his prison."*

5 | Satan's Final Rebellion & The Great White Throne Judgment

● According to Revelation 20:7, what will happen to Satan?

_____

_____

_____

_____

As we saw in Chapter 4, at Christ's Second Coming, Satan will be locked up in the Abyss for a thousand years. However, after Christ's thousand-year reign he will be released from his prison.

B.   Satan Will Deceive the Rebellious on Earth.

Not only will Satan be released at the end of the thousand-year reign of Christ, he will also work like never before to try to overthrow God. However, there is nothing new in what he will do. John predicted what Satan's strategy will be in his war against God.

> Revelation 20:7-8 (NIV)
> 7) *"When the thousand years are over, Satan will be released from his prison*
> 8) *and will go out to deceive the nations in the four corners of the earth—Gog and Magog—to gather them for battle. In number they are like the sand on the seashore.*

Satan's Final Rebellion & The Great White Throne Judgment

• According to Revelation 20:8, what will Satan do once he is released?

_____

_____

_____

_____

One thousand years of Satan's inprisonment will not change him in the least. He will still have an evil, burning desire to defeat God and have mankind worship him. Satan, still drunk with pride and self-deception, will make one final attempt at overthrowing God.

• According to Revelation 20:8 who will Satan deceive at the end of the thousand-year reign of Christ?

_____

_____

_____

All those who entered into the thousand-year reign of Christ will have believed in Him. But over the thousand years, generation upon generation of new people will be born and live under Christ's rule. People who live during the Millennium will still have sin natures. Some choose to follow Christ out of a deep desire to love Him and obey Him. But there are others who will only appear to serve Christ. Deep in the hearts of these people will be sin and rebellion towards Jesus. The rebellious people who will live during the Millennium will benefit from Christ's love and goodness, but inwardly will refuse to follow Him. God, in His wisdom, will allow Satan to roam the earth to test the hearts of those living in the Millennium. Amazingly, tens of millions of people will follow Satan in a rebellion against God.

Satan's Final Rebellion & The Great White Throne Judgment | 5

C. Satan and the Rebellious People Will Declare War Against God and Be Defeated.

As sad as it will seem, tens of millions of people moved by Satan himself will march on Jerusalem in an attempt to destroy Jesus and set-up their own kingdom. This last war against God will be absolutely futile and end in disaster for those in rebellion to Christ. John spoke of this disaster in Revelation 20:9-10—

Revelation 20:9-10 (NIV)
9) *"They marched across the breadth of the earth and surrounded the camp of God's people, the city he loves. But fire came down from heaven and devoured them.*
10) *And the devil, who deceived them, was thrown into the lake of burning sulfur, where the beast and the false prophet had been thrown. They will be tormented day and night for ever and ever."*

● According to Revelation 20:9, how are those who are in rebellion against Christ defeated by God?

_____

_____

_____

_____

5 | Satan's Final Rebellion & The Great White Throne Judgment

● According to Revelation 20:10, how will Satan be judged by God?

_____

_____

_____

_____

At long last, Satan will be throw into Hell itself. There he will be locked up forever with the Antichrist and the False Prophet. The Bible says that Satan will be "tormented day and night for ever and ever." There is no way that Satan could ever be changed from his evil and wicked ways to anything that is good. And there is no way that God's holiness and justice will ever change to let Satan into Heaven. Therefore, Satan will be locked away in Hell for ever and must pay for his horrible sins against a holy God.

II. AT THE GREAT WHITE THRONE, CHRIST WILL PASS FINAL JUDGMENT ON ALL THOSE WHO HAVE REJECTED HIM.

At last the mighty Judge, Jesus Christ, will open court proceedings to every person who has rejected Him as Savior. What an incredible but tragic time that will be. It will be a time of sadness, regret, and grief unparalleled in eternal history. Jesus will sit on His throne and be the mighty Judge that He was destined to be. The Bible says of Him in John 5:22—

John 5:22 (NIV)
"Moreover, the Father judges no one, but has entrusted all judgment to the Son,"

What a moment it will be in eternal history when Jesus Christ, the person most ignored, laughed at, and rejected by mankind, will ultimately judge those who have rejected Him. In that day no one will be able to rationalize or talk their way out of even one sin committed against God. They will have to look into the eyes of Jesus and give an account for every wrong they have ever done. The Bible tells us about this in Romans 14:12—

Romans 14:12 (TLB)
"Yes, each of us will give an account of himself to God."

Satan's Final Rebellion & The Great White Throne Judgment

The apostle John saw this great moment in a vision described in Revelation 20:11-15 when he saw Christ sitting on a Great White Throne—

Revelation 20:11-15 (NIV)

11) "Then I saw a great white throne and Him who was seated on it. Earth and sky fled from His presence, and there was no place for them.

12) And I saw the dead, great and small, standing before the throne, and books were opened. Another book was opened, which is the book of life. The dead were judged according to what they had done as recorded in the books.

13) The sea gave up the dead that were in it, and death and Hades gave up the dead that were in them, and each person was judged according to what he had done.

14) Then death and Hades were thrown into the lake of fire. The lake of fire is the second death.

15) If anyone's name was not found written in the book of life, he was thrown into the lake of fire."

A.   At the Great White Throne Judgment, Earth and Sky Will Be Destroyed by Fire.

John saw a vision of a Great White Throne and saw a person seated on it. As we have already seen, that person can be none other than Jesus Christ (John 5:22, Acts 10:42). While the Bible does not tell us exactly where these proceedings will take place, we know that they will take place somewhere suspended in space.

● John tells us that something amazing will take place. He said, "earth and sky fled from His presence and there was no place for them." What do you think John was talking about?

_____

_____

_____

5 | Satan's Final Rebellion & The Great White Throne Judgment

The Great White Throne judgment will be the final judgment for all sin. The earth and the sky have been polluted due to man and Satan's sin. Therefore Christ will judge and burn the earth itself so that all impurities will be done away with forever. The apostle Peter spoke of that incredible burning and cleansing in 2 Peter 3:10; 12b-13—

> 2 Peter 3:10; 12b-13 (NIV)
> 10) *"But the day of the Lord will come like a thief. The heavens will disappear with a roar; the elements will be destroyed by fire, and the earth and everything in it will be laid bare.*
> 12b) *...That day will bring about the destruction of the heavens by fire, and the elements will melt in the heat.*
> 13) *But in keeping his promise we are looking forward to a new heaven and a new earth, the home of righteousness."*

B. At the Great White Throne Judgment, Every Unbeliever Will Stand Before Christ.

John saw a mass of humanity standing before the Great White Throne. He said in Revelation 20:12a;13a—

> Revelation 20:12a, 13a (NIV)
> 12a) *"And I saw the dead, great and small, standing before the throne....*
> 13a) *The sea gave up the dead that were in it, and death and Hades gave up the dead that were in them ...."*

Satan's Final Rebellion & The Great White Throne Judgment

5

● According to Revelation 20:12a & 13a, who will stand before God?

_____

_____

_____

_____

John is absolutely clear that every person who has sinned against God and rejected His Son Jesus Christ will be there at the Great White Throne. He said that he "saw the dead" there. By the time the Great White Throne Judgment takes place, every unbeliever will have already died. John goes on to describe some of these dead people. Some will be great and some will be small. The great people standing there will be those who were famous and powerful in this world who openly and defiantly rebelled against God. These will be people like Hitler, Stalin, Alexander the Great, Pilate, John Lennon, Shirley MacLaine, Kurt Cobain, Mao Sung Tung.

PROJECT—Famous People Who Will Be At The Great White Throne

List some of the Famous and Powerful People you think will stand before God at the Great White Throne.

_____

_____

_____

_____

5 | Satan's Final Rebellion & The Great White Throne Judgment

John predicted that not only the great would stand before Christ at the Great White Throne but also the small. Who do you think the small will be?

_____

_____

_____

_____

The small will be the faceless billions who have lived out their lives in obscurity. Outside of immediate family and a few friends, these people are unknown. Nonetheless they are not unknown to God who saw every selfish, petty, spiteful, and cheap sin they have ever committed. These people lived basically unknown and died unknown and yet like the great, refused to give their lives to Christ.

PROJECT—Less-Famous People Who Will Be At The Great White Throne

List some of the less-famous people you think will stand before the Great White Throne. (Friends, neighbors, relatives)

_____

_____

_____

_____

Satan's Final Rebellion & The Great White Throne Judgment | 5

C. At the Great White Throne Judgment, the Books Will Be Opened.

In his vision, the apostle John saw the Judge, Jesus Christ, open up two sets of books. Outside of the Bible, no books have ever existed that are more important than these. Every person's fate for eternity will be set by what is written in those books. John spoke of this in Revelation 20:12-13b—

> Revelation 20:12-13b (NIV)
> *12) "And I saw the dead, great and small, standing before the throne, and books were opened. Another book was opened, which is the book of life. The dead were judged according to what they had done as recorded in the books.*
> *13b)...and each person was judged according to what he had done."*

- According to Revelation 20:12, John saw that "books were opened." What do you think those books are?

_____

_____

_____

_____

Satan's Final Rebellion & The Great White Throne Judgment

Satan's Final Rebellion & The Great White Throne Judgment

John explained that one set of books Jesus opened was a record of all that each individual had done or failed to do while living on this earth. God in His all-knowing mind has recorded and written in volumes of books every thought, motive, and deed ever done by mankind. From the smallest of sins to the greatest, these are all described in detail in these books. In that day, as Christ looks into the books, there will be nothing kept hidden or secret. The Bible talks about this in Hebrews 4:13—

> Hebrews 4:13 (NIV)
> *"Nothing in all creation is hidden from God's sight. Everything is uncovered and laid bare before the eyes of Him to whom we must give account."*

John talked about another book that Christ opened. He called it the "book of life." He said in Revelation 20:15—

> Revelation 20:15 (NIV)
> *"If anyone's name was not found written in the book of life, he was thrown into the lake of fire."*

● According to Revelation 20:15, what do you think the book of life is?

_____

_____

_____

_____

The Book of Life will be opened at the Great White Throne Judgment. This incredible book will have the names of every person who has ever trusted Christ as their personal Savior. If that person's name is found in the book of life they will be guaranteed a place in Heaven.

- According to Revelation 20:15, what will happen to those whose names are not found written in the book of life?

_____

_____

_____

_____

Those whose names are not found written in the book of life will, without exception, be thrown into the lake of fire. The Bible says that it will be the final place where man will dwell forever apart from God.

IN CONCLUSION

God is a perfectly holy God who must judge and punish anything that is unholy. Only through Christ can one face a holy God. The Bible says that God will throw death, Hades, and those who do not know Christ into the lake of fire. It is obvious that the most important thing we can ever do is to make sure that our names are written in the Book of Life. As a result, we will never have to face the Great White Throne Judgment but will live with Christ forever in Heaven. But those who refuse to turn to Christ, they will without exception face the Great White Throne Judgment. The prophet Daniel long ago predicted the awesomeness and finality of that judgment when he wrote—

Daniel 7:9-10 (NIV)

9) "As I looked, thrones were set in place, and the Ancient of Days took his seat. His clothing was as white as snow; the hair of his head was white like wool. His throne was flaming with fire, and its wheels were all ablaze.
10) A river of fire was flowing, coming out from before Him. Thousands upon thousands attended Him; ten thousand times ten thousand stood before him. The court was seated, and the books were opened."

---

6 The Eternal Punishment of Hell

6 | The Eternal Punishment of Hell

Those who have rejected Christ must face Him at the Great White Throne Judgment. At this judgment it will be a time of guilt, regret, and terror because on that day mankind will be sent to eternal judgment. The apostle John spoke of this judgment in Revelation 20:13-15—

Revelation 20:13-15 (NIV)
13) "The sea gave up the dead that were in it, and death and Hades gave up the dead that were in them, and each person was judged according to what he had done.
14) Then death and Hades were thrown into the lake of fire. The lake of fire is the second death.
15) If anyone's name was not found written in the book of life, he was thrown into the lake of fire."

The apostle John tells us that those who do not know Christ will be thrown into the "lake of fire." One of the most difficult things to talk about from the Bible is the whole concept of Hell. It is hard for all of us to comprehend the eternal judgment God has planned for those who reject Jesus Christ. There are those who deny the reality of Hell. Still others try to explain it away. Some people try to come up with their own ending to life and paint a far rosier picture than God has. But God wants us to look into His Word and see what He says about eternal judgment. It is in God's Word that the truth about Eternity is found.

6 The Eternal Punishment of Hell

IN THIS CHAPTER WE WILL DISCUSS
WHAT REVELATION 20:13-15 TELLS US
ABOUT THE ETERNAL JUDGMENT GOD
HAS PLANNED FOR THOSE WHO
REJECT JESUS CHRIST.

The Eternal Punishment of Hell | 6

I. IN REVELATION 20:13-15, GOD TELLS US ABOUT A HORRIBLE PLACE CALLED HADES.

Hundreds of millions of people will stand before the Great White Throne. Some of these people who will be at the Great White Throne Judgment will have been dead for thousands of years. Even though they have been dead for some length of time, they still will not have faced the "lake of fire" which John calls the "second death." We know that when a person dies they do not go out of existence. Their soul leaves their body and goes somewhere while their body remains in the grave. John tells us in Revelation 20:13-15 that the souls of those who die apart from Christ first go to a place called Hades—

> Revelation 20:13-15 (NIV)
> *13) "The sea gave up the dead that were in it, and death and **Hades** gave up the dead that were in them, and each person was judged according to what he had done.*
> *14) Then death and **Hades** were thrown into the lake of fire. The lake of fire is the second death.*
> *15) If anyone's name was not found written in the book of life, he was thrown into the lake of fire."*

● According to Revelation 20:13, John says that "death and Hades gave up the dead that were in them." What do you think death and Hades means?

_____

_____

_____

John seems to be teaching that there will be some kind of bodily resurrection. At this resurrection, the souls of all unbelievers, which will be held in Hades, will be reunited with its body to stand before Christ at the Great White Throne.

The Eternal Punishment of Hell | 6

A. What Is Hades?

Hades is a temporary place where those who have rejected Christ and have died are confined until the Great White Throne Judgment. It is a place that is hidden, gloomy and full of suffering. Every day Hades is being populated with those who have rejected Christ and have died. Jesus spoke of a place called Hades when He said in Matthew 11:23-24—

> Matthew 11:23-24 (NAS)
> *23) "And you, Capernaum, will not be exalted to heaven, will you? You shall descend to **Hades**; for if the miracles had occurred in Sodom which occurred in you, it would have remained to this day.*
> *24) Nevertheless I say to you that it shall be more tolerable for the land of Sodom in the day of judgment, than for you."*

B. What Is Hades Like?

Jesus told an amazing parable that helps explain to us more clearly where a person goes after he dies and what this place is like. In this parable found in Luke 16, Jesus told a story about a poor man who died whose name was Lazarus. Lazarus was a man who loved God and went to a place called "Paradise" or "Abraham's Bosom." The rich man however did not believe in God and went to Hades. Jesus told the story by saying in Luke 16:19-31—

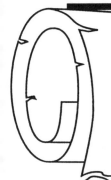

6 The Eternal Punishment of Hell

Luke 16:19-31 (TEV)

19) "There was once a rich man who dressed in the most expensive clothes and lived in great luxury every day.
20) There was also a poor man named Lazarus, covered with sores, who used to be brought to the rich man's door,
21) hoping to eat the bits of food that fell from the rich man's table. Even the dogs would come and lick his sores.
22) The poor man died and was carried by the angels to sit beside Abraham at the feast in heaven. The rich man died and was buried,
23) and in Hades, where he was in great pain, he looked up and saw Abraham, far away, with Lazarus at his side.
24) So he called out, 'Father Abraham! Take pity on me, and send Lazarus to dip his finger in some water and cool off my tongue, because I am in great pain in this fire!'
25) But Abraham said, 'Remember, my son, that in your lifetime you were given all the good things, while Lazarus got all the bad things. But now he is enjoying himself here, while you are in pain.

At Death, Unbelievers go to Hades

● At the end of verse 22 the Bible says that the rich man died and was buried but went on to a place called Hades.

In Hades, People are Conscious

● We find from verse 23 that in Hades people are conscious of themselves and others.

Hades is a Place of Great Suffering

● Verse 24 tells us that Hades is a place of great suffering because people will be in fire.

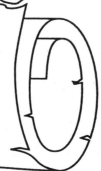

26) Besides all that, there is a deep pit lying between us, so that those who want to cross over from here to you cannot do so, nor can anyone cross over to us from where you are.'

27) The rich man said, 'Then I beg you, father Abraham, send Lazarus to my father's house,

28) where I have five brothers. Let him go and warn them so that they, at least, will not come to this place of pain.'

29) Abraham said, 'Your brothers have Moses and the prophets to warn them; your brothers should listen to what they say.'

30) The rich man answered, 'That is not enough, father Abraham! But if someone were to rise from death and go to them, then they would turn from their sins.'

31) But Abraham said, 'If they will not listen to Moses and the prophets, they will not be convinced even if someone were to rise from death.'

There is No Escape from Hades
● Verse 26 tells us that there is no way a person can get out of the prison of Hades. This verse makes it clear that there are no second chances to accept Christ once a person has died.

Hades Is So Awful, People in it Want to Warn their Loved Ones
● From verses 27 and 28 we learn that Hades is such an awful place that those in it will not want their loved ones to have to go there.

In Hades, the Truth about Sin will be Known and Felt
● Verse 30 tells us that in Hades people will gain a clearer understanding of the awfulness of the consequences of sin.

As we just saw in Luke 16:19-31, even though Hades is only a place of temporary confinement that in no way minimizes the awfulness of it. In fact it is so awful that no one would want to go there. In Hades, the pain and suffering will be so great that those there will think that it could not get any worse. The terrible reality is that those who are in Hades will one day be transferred to the "lake of fire" where they will spend eternity suffering in great pain.

II. IN REVELATION 20:14-15, GOD TELLS US THAT THOSE WHOSE NAMES ARE NOT FOUND WRITTEN IN THE BOOK OF LIFE WILL BE THROWN INTO THE LAKE OF FIRE—ALSO KNOWN AS HELL.

The Bible tells us that at the Great White Throne Judgment those who have rejected Christ will finally be thrown into the lake of fire. Scripture is clear that those thrown into the lake of fire, Hell, will be there for an eternity with no chance to ever escape. No one likes to talk about Hell. To think about it makes one shudder and wonder about the fairness of it all. Most everybody likes to think of Christ's gentle statements such as "love your neighbor as yourself." Yet in the Bible no one spoke more than Jesus of God's judgment and Hell. For example:

-Of the words spoken by Jesus that were recorded in the New Testament, 13% are about judgment and Hell. Christ spoke more of these two topics than any other.
-Of the 40 parables Jesus told in the Bible, more than half of them relate to God's eternal judgment of sinners.
-Of the 12 times that the word "Gehenna," the strongest biblical word for Hell, appears in the New Testament, there is only one which did not come from the lips of Jesus.[1]

Therefore for us to ignore or reject the truth about Judgment and Hell is to reject the very teachings of Jesus Christ. John himself in his great vision in Revelation 20 mentions the lake of fire (Hell) 3 times.

Revelation 20:14-15 (NIV)
*14) "Then death and Hades were thrown into the **lake of fire**. The **lake of fire** is the second death.*
*15) If anyone's name was not found written in the book of life, he was thrown into the **lake of fire**."*

---

[1] John Blanchard, *Whatever Happened To Hell?* (Durham England: Evangelical Press, 1993), pp128-129.

The Eternal Punishment of Hell

The Eternal Punishment of Hell

A.   What Is the Lake of Fire?

The "lake of fire" is another name for what the Bible calls Hell. John calls the lake of fire, "the second death." Death in the Bible means separation. Therefore "the second death" means the final separation from God and all that is good. The "lake of fire" or Hell, will be a place of intense suffering totally apart from God.

Defining Hell through the Words of Jesus

Jesus used a powerful Greek word when He spoke of Hell. He used the word "Gehenna." Gehenna is mentioned 12 times in the New Testament. And of the 12 times, 11 of those times came from the lips of Christ.

In Hebrew, "Gehenna" meant the "valley of Hinnom." It was a valley located south of Jerusalem where in Old Testament times horrible human sacrifices took place (2 Chronicles 33:6; Jeremiah 7:31). At the time of Christ's life, Gehenna was a city dump. It was a place where not only garbage but also the carcasses of animals and the bodies of criminals were dumped. Because the garbage and decaying bodies smelled so horribly the city dump was constantly burning. As one writer put it, "it was a place where the fires never stopped burning and the worms never stopped eating." [2]

Take all the shame, filth, hate, and suffering imaginable and one would still not have touched the depths of Hell. Our finite minds cannot grasp its awfulness. While we cannot know all the horrible depths of the sufferings of Hell, God does tell us what we need to know about it—so that we will do all in our power to avoid such a place.

B.   What Is Hell Like?

Our minds cannot comprehend the utter awfulness of eternal judgment in Hell. But what the Bible does tell us about Hell, and what our minds can comprehend about this place leaves us shuttering yet thankful that no Christian will spend even a minute there. With this in mind, let us take a quick glimpse into that awful place called Hell.

---

[2] John Blanchard, *Whatever Happened to Hell?* (Durham England: Evangelical Press, 1993), p. 41.

The Eternal Punishment of Hell

What Does the Bible Tell Us About Hell?

1. Those in Hell will be Forever Separated from the Presence of God.

There is no better definition of Hell than to say "it is a place where God is not." It staggers our minds to think of a place where God is not. For all of our lives we have benefitted from God's presence. The Bible says that Heaven and Earth are filled with His presence (Jeremiah 23:23-24). It seems all but impossible to grasp what a place would be like without the presence of God. Yet the Bible tells us that this is exactly what Hell will be like. Paul tells us in 2 Thessalonians 1:8-9—

---

2 Thessalonians 1:8-9 (TLB)
8) *"...bringing judgment on those who do not wish to know God and who refuse to accept His plan to save them through our Lord Jesus Christ.*
9) *They will be punished in everlasting hell, forever separated from the Lord, never to see the glory of his power."*

• According to 2 Thessalonians 1:8, who are the people that God will judge?

_____

_____

_____

_____

• According to 2 Thessalonians 1:9, how long will these people suffer?

_____

_____

_____

The Eternal Punishment of Hell

- According to 2 Thessalonians 1:9, how will those who refuse to turn to Christ be punished?

_____

_____

_____

_____

- What do you think it means when it says those in hell "will be forever separated from the Lord, never to see the glory of His power?"

_____

_____

_____

_____

What a terrible day that will be. When all of those who have rejected Christ will be forever separated from God, never to enjoy all the good things He has done. The Bible tells us that God causes "His sun to rise on the evil and the good, and sends rain on the righteous and the unrighteous." (Matthew 5:45). But in Hell the punished will have none of the benefits of God's presence. The people in Hell will be those who wanted God out of their lives. In Hell, they will finally get their wish.

PROJECT —
LIFE WITHOUT THE PRESENCE OF GOD

It is all but impossible to know what life without God would be like. But in this project let us try to comprehend what it would be like. Using what you know about God and realizing that none of His qualities or gifts will be in Hell, complete the project below:

Quality of God	**Without God's Quality**
Since God is Love	there will be no love in Hell
Since God is peace	there will be no peace in Hell
Since God is light	there will be no light in Hell
Since God is order	Hell will be full of confusion
Since God is Holy	_____

_____

_____

_____

_____

_____

The Eternal Punishment of Hell | 6

2. Those in Hell will be in Outer Darkness.

No doubt you have heard people say that Hell won't be so bad. The reason they say this is because they feel all their friends will be there, and therefore they will be in good company. Those who believe this have never understood Christ's description of Hell. Jesus called Hell—"outer darkness." Speaking of outer darkness Jesus said in Matthew 8:12—

> Matthew 8:12 (TLB)
> *"And many an Israelite—those for whom the Kingdom was prepared—shall be cast into **outer darkness**, into the place of weeping and torment."*

- According to Matthew 8:12, what do you think the Jesus meant when He described Hell as "outer darkness?"

_____

_____

_____

_____

When Christ spoke of the "outer darkness" He was referring to a place that is so far away from anything that is familiar to us it is unimaginable. Just as believers will feel at home when they get to Heaven, so those who reject Christ will be thrown into a hostile, brutal, and savage environment. Not only that but it will be pitch black. They will be caught up in a darkness unlike anything they have ever ever experienced. The idea of being trapped in unfamiliar surroundings covered in the blackest darkness is horribly frightening. Job described this darkness in Job 10:21b-22—

The Eternal Punishment of Hell

> Job 10:21b-22 (NIV)
> *21) "...to the land of gloom and deep shadow,*
> *22) to the land of deepest night, of deep shadow and disorder, where even the light is like darkness."*

3. Those in Hell will be Imprisoned with Other Horrible Beings.

It will become obvious to those in Hell that they are truly locked away. Most prisoners of today at least have the hope of being paroled or somehow escaping their predicament. But those in Hell will be locked in darkness, misery and fear and will have no such hope. They will be left with the finality of their pain and regrets. The Bible speaks of being locked away in Hell in 2 Peter 2:4 where Peter describes how God dealt with fallen angels:

> 2 Peter 2:4 (TLB)
> *"For God did not spare even the angels who sinned, but threw them into hell, chained in gloomy caves and darkness until the judgment day."*

• According to 2 Peter 2:4, what did God do to these angels who sinned?

_____

_____

_____

_____

The Eternal Punishment of Hell | 6

The Bible tells us that some of the fallen angels or demons were immediately locked away for the day of judgment. If these demons, who are much more powerful than you and I, cannot escape God's judgment of being locked up in Hell, then no man or woman who rejects Jesus Christ will stand a chance of escaping this eternal prison.

Those in Hell will have the terror of knowing that they are locked away for ever. But that will only be part of their pain. Each person in Hell will be around the most repulsive beings in eternity. Some of these repulsive beings include Satan, demons, the Antichrist and the False Prophet (Matthew 25:41; Revelation 20:10). Since every person in Hell is without the presence of God, they will be reduced to the lowest of desires and actions. Prisons today are not awful simply because of bars and confinement, they are awful because one is locked away with others who are vile and treacherous. The Bible in Revelation 21:8 talks about some of those who will be thrown into Hell—

> Revelation 21:8 (NIV)
> *"But the cowardly, the unbelieving, the vile, the murderers, the sexually immoral, those who practice magic arts, the idolaters and all liars—their place will be in the fiery lake of burning sulfur. This is the second death."*

● According to Revelation 21:8, who are some of the people who will be in Hell?

_____

_____

_____

No one knows for sure how beings in Hell will relate to one another. However it will happen, it will make Hell an even more horrible place than one could have ever imagined in their worst nightmare.

The Eternal Punishment of Hell

4. Those in Hell will Face Unquenchable Fire and Eternal Suffering.

When Jesus described the awfulness of Hell, He most often spoke of it as fire. For example, He said in Matthew 18:8-9—

> Matthew 18:8-9 (NCV)
> 8) *"If your hand or your foot causes you to sin, cut if off and throw it away. It is better for you to lose part of your body and live forever than to have two hands and two feet and be thrown into the fire that burns forever. 9) If your eye causes you to sin, take it out and throw it away. It is better for you to have only one eye and live forever than to have two eyes and be thrown into the fire of hell."*

- According to Matthew 18:8-9, what does Jesus say about our hands, feet, and eyes?

_____

_____

_____

_____

- According to Matthew 18:8-9, do you think Jesus is telling us to literally cut off our hands, or feet, or eyes if they cause us to sin?

_____

_____

_____

_____

The Eternal Punishment of Hell

6 The Eternal Punishment of Hell

No one understands the awfulness of sin like Jesus Christ. It was the horror of sin that demanded of Him the greatest sacrifice in all eternity. Jesus is not suggesting that we cut off our hands or feet or pluck out our eyes when we sin. But He wants us to understand this: Sin is so awful that it separates us from God and failure to understand this puts us in danger of the eternal fire of Hell. However, those who give their lives to Christ have their sins forgiven and need not fear the eternal fire of Hell.

The Bible also speaks of the eternal fire of Hell in Revelation 20:10—

Revelation 20:10 (NIV)
"And the devil, who deceived them, was thrown into the lake of burning sulfur, where the beast and the false prophet had been thrown. They will be tormented day and night for ever and ever."

• How long will those suffer who are in the lake of burning sulfur?

_____

_____

_____

_____

Being severely burned is one of the most painful experiences known to man. But in Hell, the burning will never stop.

The Eternal Punishment of Hell

PROJECT—BEING BURNED BADLY

Describe a time in your life when you had a bad burn. Maybe you were out in the sun too long; or you put your hand on a hot stove. In any case what was it like?

_____

_____

_____

_____

No matter how awful your experience of burning was, it does not come close to the eternal pain and suffering that will go on in Hell. Jesus did not hold back from explaining the experiences of people and their sufferings in the eternal place of judgment. He spoke of this in Matthew 13:49-50—

Matthew 13:49-50 (NIV)
49) *"This is how it will be at the end of the age. The angels will come and separate the wicked from the righteousness*
50) *and throw them into the fiery furnace, where there will be weeping and gnashing of teeth."*

• According to Matthew 13:50, what will people be doing in Hell?

_____

_____

_____

_____

The Eternal Punishment of Hell

The Eternal Punishment of Hell

The Bible says that people in Hell will be weeping. Their tears will never stop. Never in their wildest dreams could they have ever imagined that they would have gotten themselves into this predicament. They will be left with their pain and their regrets. Their agony will be so great that they will grind their teeth as they grimace in pain. It is terrible to say, but this punishment will last forever. The apostle John, writing in Revelation 14:11, in a vision saw a glimpse of how awful it would be —

> Revelation 14:11 (TLB)
> *"The smoke of their torture rises forever and ever, they will have no relief day or night...."*

IN CONCLUSION

Thinking about Hell is an emotionally-painful experience. So difficult is it that few people even dare to ponder on it. Most non-Christians think that it is impossible that a loving God would send anyone to eternal Hell. Yet the Bible is clear: Hell awaits everyone who does not give their lives to Christ. God, of all beings, knows the horribleness of Hell. He knows that His holiness cannot tolerate any sin whatsoever. He also knows that sin is so awful that it must be judged for all eternity. That is why He was willing to send His Son to die on the Cross for us to take that Hell upon Himself so that we could go free. God does not send anyone to Hell. Each person chooses to go there of his own free will. God does not send people to Hell with some kind of sick vengeance, but with a broken heart. He realizes that there is no other way to deal with the awful sin of those who reject God's gift of Jesus Christ.

> 2 Corinthians 5:11 (NKJV)
> *"Knowing, therefore, the terror of the Lord, we persuade men;"*

Heaven—Our Forever Home

7 | Heaven— Our Forever Home

Hell will be horrible. But Heaven will be just the opposite. Hell cannot be imagined in its awfulness and Heaven cannot be imagined for its beauty, pleasure and greatness. The Bible is clear that for those who have made peace with God through Christ there is but one destiny; and that is Heaven. The apostle Paul spoke of our future in Philippians 3:20—

> Philippians 3:20 (NIV)
> *"But our citizenship is in heaven. And we eagerly await a Savior from there, the Lord Jesus Christ,"*

Although the Bible talks a lot about Heaven, it is very difficult for our small minds to grasp its greatness. Heaven is so great that there is nothing in our lives to compare it to. It is beyond our wildest imagination for its incredibleness. The Bible speaks of this in 1 Corinthians 2:9b—

> 1 Corinthians 2:9b (NIV)
> *"...No eye has seen, no ear has heard, no mind has conceived what God has prepared for those who love Him"*

Yet God in His love has given us a glimpse of what Heaven will be like. And what little we can understand about Heaven moves us to hope, joy, and an awe beyond anything we can imagine.

Heaven—Our Forever Home

IN THIS CHAPTER WE WILL SEEK TO
GRASP SOME OF THE INCREDIBLE
TRUTHS ABOUT HEAVEN THAT GOD
HAS REVEALED TO US IN HIS WORD.

Heaven—Our Forever Home

I. THE BIBLE TELLS US THAT THERE WILL BE A NEW HEAVEN AND A NEW EARTH WHERE WE WILL BE PERFECTLY SATISFIED.

Jesus made a promise 2,000 years ago to His disciples. He said in John 14:1-3

> John 14:1-3 (NIV)
> 1) *"Do not let your hearts be troubled. Trust in God; trust also in me.*
> 2) *In my Father's house are many rooms; if it were not so, I would have told you. I am going there to prepare a place for you.*
> 3) *And if I go and prepare a place for you, I will come back and take you to be with me that you also may be where I am."*

Jesus clearly taught that He is preparing a place for us. This place is Heaven. For 2,000 years now Jesus Christ, with His incredible creating powers (Colossians 1:16) has been at work making a new home for us. What He has built for us in Heaven is new, awesome, and all that we will ever need for an eternity of pleasure, peace, and joy.

A. In Heaven, Everything will be New.

The apostle John saw a vision of Heaven. He wrote of what He saw in this vision in Revelation 21:1—

> Revelation 21:1 (NIV)
> *"Then I saw a new heaven and a new earth, for the first heaven and the first earth had passed away, and there was no longer any sea."*

7 | Heaven—Our Forever Home

• According to Revelation 21:1, what do you think John meant when he said, "I saw a new heaven and a new earth?"

_____

_____

_____

_____

• According to Revelation 21:1, what do you think John means when He said "the first heavens and the first earth have passed away?"

_____

_____

_____

_____

The word "new" refers to a brand new creation, different from anything now known. The new heaven and new earth will be different from the heavens and earth we now have. For example there will be no sea on the new earth. The world's oceans are crucial to life on our planet. The world's seas help regulate the climate, wind, and oxygen. Without them, the world as we now know it could not exist. Somehow on this new earth life will sustain itself without any sea. The new earth will operate differently from anything we now understand. Isaiah spoke of how marvelous, new, and different the new heaven and new earth will be in Isaiah 65:17—

> Isaiah 65:17 (NIV)
> *"Behold, I will create new heavens and a new earth. The former things will not be remembered, nor will they come to mind."*

- According to Isaiah 65:17, what do you think Isaiah means when God said, "I will create new heavens and a new earth?"

_____

_____

_____

Some people believe that the earth and the heavens we now have will merely undergo a "cosmic make-over." However the Bible states that "the first heavens and the first earth have passed away." The word "passed away" means to "come to an end, to perish." The Bible talks about the passing away of the heavens and the earth in 2 Peter 3:7; 10; 12b-13—

> 2 Peter 3:7; 10; 12b-13 (NIV)
> *7) "By the same word the present heavens and earth are reserved for fire, being kept for the day of judgment and destruction of ungodly men.*
> *10) But the day of the Lord will come like a thief. The heavens will disappear with a roar; the elements will be destroyed by fire, and the earth and everything in it will be laid bare....*
> *12b) That day will bring about the destruction of the heavens by fire, and the elements will melt in the heat.*
> *13) But in keeping with His promise we are looking forward to a new heaven and a new earth, the home of righteousness."*

Heaven—Our Forever Home

B.   In Heaven, We Will be Perfectly Satisfied.

In Chapter 6 we said that what makes Hell so terrible is the total absence of God. But what will make Heaven such a magnificent place is that we will be in the very presence of God Himself. All Christians know of God's presence now. But in Heaven, we will be closer to Him and more intimate with Him than we could ever possibly imagine. John spoke of this in Revelation 21:3-4—

Revelation 21:3-4 (NIV)
3) "And I heard a loud voice from the throne saying, 'Now the dwelling of God is with men, and He will live with them. They will be His people, and God Himself will be with them and be their God.
4) He will wipe every tear from their eyes. There will be no more death or mourning or crying or pain, for the old order of things has passed away."

• According to Revelation 21:3, in Heaven how close will God be to us?

_____

_____

_____

_____

Heaven—Our Forever Home

John tells us that God will actually dwell with us and live with us in Heaven. When the Bible says that God will dwell with us it literally means "to tabernacle" or "headquarter." In Heaven there will be a whole new kind of existence. Up until this time the intense presence of God, where His very essence dwells is in Heaven. Man on the other hand lives on earth. In the New Heaven and Earth, God will move His headquarters to be among His followers. Man will live and move within God's headquarters at ease. There will be a closeness between God and man that has not been possible since the Garden of Eden. This closeness of God will bring joy to those in Heaven beyond their wildest dreams.

- What do you think the Bible means when it says, "He will wipe away every tear from their eye."?

_____

_____

_____

_____

God in His compassion will remove anything from those in Heaven that would cause tears. Some may still be mourning their lost friends and relatives who are in Hell. God will remove their heartbreak forever. Still others may have powerful and painful memories of being persecuted for Christ on earth. God will help them to never remember that pain again. In Heaven, there will be no sin. Therefore all the consequences of sin will be gone as well. There will be no more crying or pain or death. There will be a whole new kind of living in Heaven. The old way of living that caused so much pain and trouble on this earth will pass away for ever.

Heaven—Our Forever Home

PROJECT —
WHAT WILL THINGS BE LIKE IN HEAVEN?

In your own words try to describe how happy you will be in Heaven.

_____

_____

_____

_____

_____

_____

II. IN HEAVEN, GOD WILL CREATE A CITY CALLED NEW JERUSALEM, AN AWESOME DISPLAY OF HIS CREATIVITY AND LOVE FOR US.

A. What is the New Jerusalem?

The apostle John saw a vision of something incredible. He saw a whole city coming down from heaven to the New Earth. He called this city the New Jerusalem. He spoke of this New Jerusalem in Revelation 21:2; 10—

Revelation 21:2; 10 (NIV)
2) *"I saw the Holy City, the New Jerusalem, coming down out of heaven from God, prepared as a bride beautifully dressed for her husband...*
10) And he (an angel) *carried me away in the Spirit to a mountain great and high, and showed me the Holy City, Jerusalem, coming down out of heaven from God."*

● According to Revelation 21:2; 10, why do you think God created a New Jerusalem?

_____

_____

_____

_____

Heaven—Our Forever Home

The name Jerusalem means "founded by God." The earthly Jerusalem was founded by God to be the center of a nation that would bring about a whole new people. The present city of Jerusalem is located in Israel. It is a city that has become a symbol of man's attempts to know God, yet is filled with the history of the failure of mankind to be what God wants them to be. The Bible tells us that Jesus Himself wept over Jerusalem because of her sins.

Matthew 23:37 (NIV)
"O Jerusalem, Jerusalem, you who kill the prophets and stone those sent to you, how often I have longed to gather your children together, as a hen gathers her chicks under her wings, but you were not willing."

In Heaven, there will be a New Jerusalem that will complete God's plan. There in that city will be all those who have loved God and are now set apart for Him forever. The New Jerusalem, untouched by sin, will be the most awesome city ever imagined. This New Jerusalem will be the Christians' home for ever and ever.

## B.	The New Jerusalem will be an Incredible City, Full of Beauty.

As mentioned earlier, Heaven will be so amazing that it is difficult to comprehend what will be there. Yet God showed John in a vision a glimpse of this awe-inspiring city called New Jerusalem.

Heaven—Our Forever Home

John's Vision of the New Jerusalem

Revelation 21:10-27 (NIV)

10) *"And he* (an angel) *carried me away in the Spirit to a mountain great and high, and showed me the Holy City, Jerusalem, coming down out of heaven from God.*

11) *It shone with the glory of God, and its brilliance was like that of a very precious jewel, like a jasper, clear as crystal.*

12) *It had a great, high wall with twelve gates, and with twelve angels at the gates. On the gates were written the names of the twelve tribes of Israel.*

13) *There were three gates on the east, three on the north, three on the south and three on the west.*

14) *The wall of the city had twelve foundations, and on them were the names of the twelve apostles of the Lamb.*

(15) *The angel who talked with me had a measuring rod of gold to measure the city, its gates and its walls.*

16) *The city was laid out like a square, as long as it was wide. He measured the city with the rod and found it to be 12,000 stadia in length, and as wide and high as it is long.*

17) *He measured its wall and it was 144 cubits thick, by man's measurement, which the angel was using.*

18) *The wall was made of jasper, and the city of pure gold, as pure as glass.*

19) *The foundations of the city walls were decorated with every kind of precious stone. The first foundation was jasper, the second sapphire, the third chalcedony, the fourth emerald,*

20) *the fifth sardonyx, the sixth carnelian, the seventh chrysolite, the eighth beryl, the ninth topaz, the tenth chrysoprase, the eleventh jacinth, and the twelfth amethyst.*

21) *The twelve gates were twelve pearls, each gate made of a single pearl. The great street of the city was of pure gold, like transparent glass.*

22) *I did not see a temple in the city, because the Lord God Almighty and the Lamb are its temple.*

23) *The city does not need the sun or the moon to shine on it, for the glory of God gives it light, and the Lamb its lamp.*

24) *The nations will walk by its light, and the kings of the earth will bring their splendor into it.*

25) *On no day will its gates ever be shut, for there will be no night there.*

26) *The glory and honor of the nations will be brought into it.*

27) *Nothing impure will ever enter it, nor will anyone who does what is shameful or deceitful, but only those whose names are written in the Lamb's book of life."*

The Enormous Size of the New Jerusalem

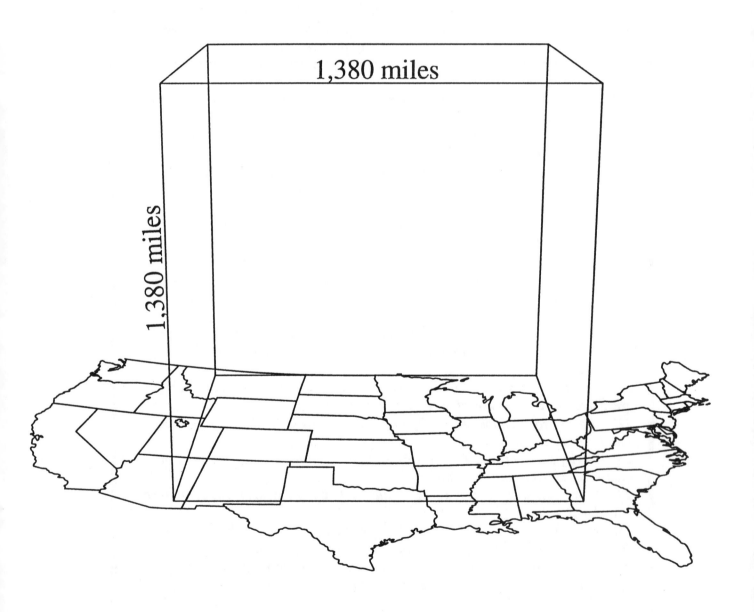

1,380 miles

1,380 miles

Heaven—Our Forever Home

1. The New Jerusalem will be the Largest City Ever Built.

Seeing the New Jerusalem will be an Eternal Awe-Inspiring experience. One will never tire of gazing at its beauty. Yet its beauty is only part of its magnificent display of God's infinite creativity. Not only will the New Jerusalem be beautiful but it will also be a Gigantic city. John spoke of its dimensions in Revelation 21:15-17—

> Revelation 21:15-17 (NIV)
> 15) *"The angel who talked with me had a measuring rod of gold to measure the city, its gates and its walls.*
> 16) *The city was laid out like a square, as long as it was wide. He measured the city with the rod and found it to be 12,000 stadia in length, and as wide and high as it is long.*
> 17) *He measured its wall and it was 144 cubits thick, by man's measurement, which the angel was using."*

The size of this gigantic city staggers our minds. John tells us that city will be laid out like a square. It will extend in length, width and height 12,000 stadia. The Greek stadia measured 607 feet, making this a distance of 1,380 miles. This would give the city a total base area of 1,904,400 square miles. And this is not counting its height which reaches 1,380 miles—far above the atmosphere into space. Some people believe that there will be several levels in the New Jerusalem. Perhaps stacking one level every mile. John also notes that the walls of the New Jerusalem are 144 cubits thick, or about 216 feet. There is nothing known to man with which he can compare this immense city.

7

Heaven—Our Forever Home

The height of the city of
New Jerusalem is so great,
to get the true perspective,
you would have to continue
this column upwards—
and you would need to put four
of these manuals together
from bottom to top to equal
the height of New Jerusalem
(scale of 3.33 inches to
100 miles)

Meteors   Mile 100 —————

Dust Belt   Mile 50 —————

Ozone Layer Mile 9 —————

Sea Level   Mile 0 —————

2. God's Beauty and Brilliance will Shine Throughout New Jerusalem.

The Beauty and Glory of God is so beyond our comprehension that it is difficult to describe. Yet John, moved along by the Holy Spirit, gives us a description we can understand. John tells us that the New Jerusalem will have God's glory and brilliance shining throughout it. He said in Revelation 21:10-11—

> Revelation 21:10-11 (NIV)
> *10) "And he* (an angel) *carried me away in the Spirit to a mountain great and high, and showed me the Holy City, Jerusalem, coming down out of heaven from God.*
> *11) It shone with the glory of God, and its brilliance was like that of a very precious jewel, like a jasper, clear as crystal."*

• According to Revelation 21:11, what do you think "jasper, clear as crystal," looks like?

_____

_____

_____

_____

Jasper, in John's day, was the most precious stone there was. The best way to describe it in today's English would be to describe it as a "giant, blue-white diamond", an overwhelmingly beautiful gem. Yet, no diamond is as beautiful as when light shines through it. God's light will sparkle through this city radiating a beautiful blue and white color.

Not only will God's brilliance shine throughout the city, but His beauty will be at the very center of it. So bright will this beautiful light be, that the New Jerusalem will need nothing else to lighten it.

Revelation 21:22-23 (NIV)
22) "I did not see a temple in the city, because the Lord God Almighty and the Lamb are its temple.
23) The city does not need the sun or the moon to shine on it, for the glory of God gives it light, and the Lamb its lamp."

● According to Revelation 21:22, why is it important that God is called the "temple of the New Jerusalem?"

_____

_____

_____

_____

In Biblical times the Temple in Jerusalem was the center of spiritual and social activity. The whole city revolved around that massive temple. In Heaven there will be no temple, for the center of activity will be God Himself. What a sight that will be! There in the center of the city of New Jerusalem will be God Himself in all His beauty. What a beautiful light will come from Him. This city will not need the sun or the moon or any electricity to light it. John said of that city in Revelation 21:23—

Heaven—Our Forever Home | 7

Revelation 21:23 (NIV)
"The city does not need the sun or the moon to shine on it, for the glory of God gives it light, and the Lamb is its lamp."

3. The Bible Gives Amazing Descriptions of the New Jerusalem.

John's vision of the New Jerusalem is on the one hand, breath-taking, yet on the other, extremely detailed. In Revelation 21:12-14; 18-21, John gives a detailed description of some of the physical features of the New Jerusalem.

Revelation 21:12-14; 18-21 (NIV)
12) "It had a great, high wall with twelve gates, and with twelve angels at the gates. On the gates were written the names of the twelve tribes of Israel.
13) There were three gates on the east, three on the north, three on the south, and three on the west.
14) The wall of the city had twelve foundations, and on them were the names of the twelve apostles of the Lamb....
18) The wall was made of jasper, and the city of pure gold, as pure as glass.
19) The foundations of the city walls were decorated with every kind of precious stone. The first foundation was jasper, the second sapphire, the third chalcedony, the fourth emerald,
20) the fifth sardonyx, the sixth carnelian, the seventh chrysolite, the eighth beryl, the ninth topaz, the tenth chrysoprase, the eleventh jacinth, and the twelfth amethyst.
21) The twelve gates were twelve pearls, each gate made of a single pearl. The great street of the city was of pure gold, like transparent glass."

Heaven—Our Forever Home

The New Jerusalem will have a High Wall made of Jasper

> Revelation 21:12a; 18a (NIV)
> *12a) "It had a great, high wall...*
> *18a) The wall was made of jasper,"*

Evidently a high wall is built around the total city. This high wall indicates to us that the city is real and has limits. John tells us that this wall is made completely of Jasper (a beautiful light-blue diamond). What an awesome sight that will be when we see the glory of God reflecting off the walls of solid Jasper.

The New Jerusalem will have Twelve Gates, each made of a Single Pearl

> Revelation 21:12-13; 21a (NIV)
> *12) "It had a great, high wall with twelve gates and with twelve angels at the gates. On the gates were written the names of the twelve tribes of Israel.*
> *13) There were three gates on the east, three on the north, three on the south and three on the west....*
> *21a) The twelve gates were twelve pearls, each gate made of a single pearl."*

The twelve gates indicate that there will be free access into and out of this city. We will be free to go out into all the New Earth and New Heavens. There are three gates on each side. Written on these gates are the names of the twelve tribes of Israel (Judah, Reuben, Gad, Asher, Naphtali, Manasseh, Simeon, Levi, Issachar, Zebulun, Joseph, Benjamin).

Heaven—Our Forever Home

John tells us of something that is truly hard to imagine: each gate will be made of a single pearl. In ancient times, a pearl was a very rare item only found among the extremely rich. It will truly be an amazing moment in eternity when we pass through those pearly gates.

The New Jerusalem will have Twelve Foundations, each Decorated with Precious Stones

Revelation 21:14; 19-20 (NIV)
14) "The wall of the city had twelve foundations, and on them were the names of the twelve apostles of the Lamb....
19) The foundations of the city walls were decorated with every kind of precious stone. The first foundation was jasper, the second sapphire, the third chalcedony, the fourth emerald,
20) the fifth sardonyx, the sixth carnelian, the seventh chrysolite, the eighth beryl, the ninth topaz, the tenth chrysoprase, the eleventh jacinth, and the twelfth amethyst."

In John's vision he tells us that there will be twelve foundations to this city. These twelve foundations each have the name of one of the twelve apostles of Jesus Christ (Peter, James, John, Andrew, Philip, Bartholomew, Matthew, Thomas, James, Thaddaeus, Simon, and Matthias). The fact that their names are engraved on the foundations makes it clear that this is to be the eternal home for all of those who have trusted Christ as Savior. But the foundations of this city are unlike any you and I have ever seen. John tells us that these foundations will be made up of precious stones. Here are a list of these precious stones.

Heaven—Our Forever Home

Precious Foundation Stones In The New Jerusalem

(1) Jasper - brilliant blue-white diamond

(2) Sapphire - the ancient sapphire was known to be a deep blue stone.

(3) Chalcedony - thought to be sky blue with other colors running through it.

(4) Emerald - is a bright, light green, transparent precious stone.

(5) Sardonyx - a red and white stone

(6) Sardius - refers to a jewel of reddish color.

(7) Chrysolyte - a transparent stone, golden in color.

(8) Beryl - is a precious stone which is sea green in color.

(9) Topaz - yellow green and transparent stone.

(10) Chrysoprasus - an apple green, fine grained stone.

(11) Jacinth - is a violet color.

(12) Amethyst - is a clear purple.

With the most precious stones known to man covering the foundations of this Holy City it will no doubt reflect the glory of God with more brilliance and color than anything man has ever seen.

Heaven—Our Forever Home

The New Jerusalem will be Made of Pure Gold

> Revelation 21:18b; 21b (NIV)
> *18b) "..and the city of pure gold, as pure as glass....*
> *21b) The great street of the city was of pure gold, like transparent glass."*

Gold is one of the most coveted of materials in the history of the world. Yet it is also one of the rarest of precious metals. But in the New Jerusalem gold will be everywhere. John tells us he saw a "city of pure gold, as pure as glass." This seems to be a description of something in the New Heaven and New Earth that is better than gold. Gold is beautiful, but it is full of impurities. Even after refining it one can still not see through it as glass. Apparently John was using human language to describe something brand new; something so much more wonderful than just gold.

Heaven—Our Forever Home

Heaven—Our Forever Home

IN CONCLUSION

The New Jerusalem will be beautiful. The precious stones will be everywhere. This gigantic city will be a display of incredible craftsmanship. It will take an eternity to be able to see and enjoy it all. And yet all of this beauty and craftsmanship will pale in comparison to the very glory of Christ that will be in full view. It is mind-boggling to know that we will be able to look into the face of Jesus and dwell on His beauty and love forever. One thing is for certain: God will never short-change those who give their lives to Jesus Christ. Out of His deep love and creativity, He will create Heaven, a place so wonderful that we will not even be able to recall what things used to be like here on earth. All of the riches of the world from the beginning of time until now would not even compare to one square inch of the awesomeness of this eternal city. It is exciting to know that in a few years we will be in Heaven.

Revelation 22:1-7 (NIV)
1) "Then the angel showed me the river of the water of life, as clear as crystal, flowing from the throne of God and of the Lamb
2) down the middle of the great street of the city. On each side of the river stood the tree of life, bearing twelve crops of fruit, yielding its fruit every month. And the leaves of the tree are for the healing of the nations.
3) No longer will there be any curse. The throne of God and of the Lamb will be in the city, and his servants will serve Him.
4) They will see His face, and His name will be on their foreheads.
5) There will be no more night. They will not need the light of a lamp or the light of the sun, for the Lord God will give them light. And they will reign for ever and ever.
6) The angel said to me, 'These words are trustworthy and true. The Lord, the God of the spirits of the prophets, sent his angel to show His servants the things that must soon take place.
7) Behold, I am coming soon! Blessed is he who keeps the words of the prophecy in this book."

Heaven—Our Forever Home

FINAL CONCLUSION
A Walk With Christ Through Eternity

It is truly amazing to understand God's eternal plan. The Bible tells us that in the end, Jesus Christ will rule triumphant over all evil. After studying these incredible events of God's eternal plan we are left asking three important questions:

1. When will Christ Return?

Of course no one knows. Maybe today. Maybe tomorrow. Maybe next year. But this much we do know—that Christ will come even as people on this earth mock us for believing in Him. The Bible speaks of this in 2 Peter 3—

---

2 Peter 3:3-4; 8-10a (TLB)

3) "First, I want to remind you that in the last days there will come scoffers who will do every wrong they can think of and laugh at the truth.
4) This will be their line of argument: 'So Jesus promised to come back, did he? Then where is he? He'll never come! Why, as far back as anyone can remember, everything has remained exactly as it was since the first day of creation...'
8) But don't forget this, dear friends, that a day or a thousand years from now is like tomorrow to the Lord.
9) He isn't really being slow about His promised return, even though it sometimes seems that way. But He is waiting, for the good reason that He is not willing that any should perish, and He is giving more time for sinners to repent.
10) The day of the Lord is surely coming, as unexpectedly as a thief."

---

2. Have You Settled the Question of Where You will Spend Eternity?

The most important question in eternity is a question that Pilate asked the crowd in Matthew 27:22—

> Matthew 27:22 (NCV)
> "So what should I do with Jesus, the one called the Christ?"

All of God's prophecies will come to pass. Jesus Christ will Return to this earth; He will Return in the air for His church. Will He take you with Him to Heaven? Do you know beyond a shadow of a doubt that if Christ appeared this very moment, your eternal destiny would be Heaven? The Bible says in John 3:36—

> John 3:36 (TLB)
> *"And all who trust Him—God's Son—to save them have eternal life; those who don't believe and obey Him shall never see Heaven, but the wrath of God remains upon them."*

The Bible is clear that there are only two places to spend eternity. Right now if you are unsure that your eternal destiny is Heaven, hcrc is a simple prayer you can pray:

LORD JESUS, I KNOW THAT I DESERVE THE WRATH YOU WILL BE BRINGING TO THOSE WHO REJECT YOU. BUT I THANK YOU THAT YOU LOVE ME AND DIED TO PAY THE FULL PENALTY FOR MY SIN. I ACCEPT THE FREE GIFT OF SALVATION YOU OFFER, AND I TURN AWAY FROM MY SIN AND INVITE YOU TO TAKE YOUR RIGHTFUL PLACE AS MY LORD AND SAVIOR. THANK YOU FOR GIVING ME YOUR ETERNAL LIFE

Heaven—Our Forever Home

The Bible says of those who accept Christ:

> John 5:24 (NCV)
> *"I tell you the truth, whoever hears what I say and believes in the One who sent me has eternal life. That person will not be judged guilty but has already left death and entered life."*

3. If Christ were to Return Today, Would He find You Living for Eternity—or the Things of this World?

When we set our minds on things above and lay up treasures in Heaven, we show God that we agree with Him that Heaven is what is really important. The good things we do on earth in Christ's name prompts Him to give us eternal rewards. Jesus talks about living for eternity rather than the things of this world in Matthew 6:19-21—

> Matthew 6:19-21 (NIV)
> *19) "Do not store up for yourselves treasures on earth, where moth and rust destroy, and where thieves break in and steal.*
> *20) But store up for yourselves treasures in Heaven, where moth and rust do not destroy, and where thieves do not break in and steal.*
> *21) For where your treasure is, there your heart will be also."*

Living for eternity also comes with the promise that we will be rewarded for the good things we did in Christ's power and for His glory. Jesus tells us this in Revelation 22:12—

Heaven—Our Forever Home | 7

> Revelation 22:12 (NIV)
> *"Behold, I am coming soon! My reward is with Me, and I will give to everyone according to what he has done."*

Are we who are Christians living in such a way that we won't be ashamed of ourselves when Christ comes back? How are we different from the world around us in our speech, our actions, and our attitudes?

> Philippians 2:14-16 (NIV)
> *14) "Do everything without complaining or arguing,*
> *15) so that you may become blameless and pure, children of God without fault in a crooked and depraved generation, in which you shine like stars in the universe*
> *16) as you hold out the word of life."*

As Christians we believe in a real Hell, full of eternal torment and suffering. Realizing the awfulness of the eternal punishment of Hell, Paul urges us in 2 Corinthians 5:11 to tell others about eternal life through Jesus Christ—

> 2 Corinthians 5:11 (NKJV)
> *"Knowing, therefore, the terror of the Lord, we persuade men;"*

The closing verses of the Bible encourages us with a word from Jesus Christ, and reminds us that in the meantime, God is watching out for us:

> Revelation 22:20-21 (NIV)
> *20) "He who testifies to these things says, 'Yes, I am coming soon.' Amen. Come, Lord Jesus.*
> *21) The grace of the Lord Jesus be with God's people. Amen."*

Bibliography

Blanchard, John. *Whatever Happened to Hell?* Durham, England: Evangelical Press, 1993.

Carty, Jay. *Playing with Fire: Do Nice People Really Go to Hell?* Sisters, Oregon: Multnomah Press, 1992.

Criswell, W.A. and Paige Patterson. *Heaven.* Wheaton: Tyndale House Publishers, 1991.

Crockett, William (ed.) *Four Views on Hell.* Grand Rapids: Zondervan Publishing House, 1992.

Fernando, Ajith. *Crucial Questions about Hell.* Wheaton: Crossway Books, 1991.

Graham, Billy. *Facing Death and the Life After.* Waco: Word Publishing Co., 1987.

Hendriksen, William. *The Bible on the Life Hereafter.* Grand Rapids: Baker Book House, 1959.

Hunt, Dave. *Whatever Happened to Heaven?* Eugene, Oregon: Harvest House Publishing Co., 1988.

Jeffrey, Grant R. *Heaven: The Last Frontier.* New York: Bantam Books, 1991.

Jeremiah, David. *Escape the Coming Night.* Dallas: Word Publishing Co., 1990.

Kroll, Woodrow M. *Tested By Fire.* Neptune, New Jersey: Loizeaux Brothers, 1977.

LaHaye, Tim. *How To Study Bible Prophecy for Yourself.* Eugene, Oregon: Harvest House Publishing, 1990.

LaHaye, Tim. *Revelation.* Grand Rapids: Zondervan Publishing House, 1975.

MacArthur, John. *Heaven.* Chicago: Moody Press, 1988.

MacArthur, John. *The MacArthur New Testament Commentary: 1 Corinthians.* Chicago: Moody Press, 1984.

Moody, D.L. *Heaven and How to Get There.* Chicago: Moody Press.

Pache, Rene. *The Return of Jesus Christ* translated by William S. LaSor. Chicago: Moody Press, 1955.

Pentecost, J. Dwight. *Prophecy for Today* (Revised). Grand Rapids: Discovery House Publishing, 1989.

Pentecost, J. Dwight. *Things to Come.* Grand Rapids: Zondervan Publishing House, 1958.

Phillips, John. *Exploring the Psalms* 2 volumes. Neptune, New Jersey: Loizeaux Brothers, 1988.

Phillips, John. *Exploring Revelation.* Neptune, New Jersey: Loizeaux Brothers, 1987.

Ryrie, Charles C. *Basic Theology.* Wheaton: Victor Books, 1982.

Spurgeon, C.H. *The Treasury of David* 3 volumes. Peabody, Mass.: Hendrickson Publishers.

Stedman, Ray C. *God's Final Word.* Grand Rapids: Discovery House Publishers, 1991.

Tan, Paul L. *Encyclopedia of 7700 Illustrations: Signs of the Times.* Rockville, Maryland: Assurance Publishers, 1979.

Tan, Paul L. *The New Jerusalem.* Rockville, Maryland: Assurance Publishers, 1978.

Van Impe, Jack. *Your Future: An A-Z Index to Prophecy.* Troy, Michigan: Jack Van Impe Ministries, 1989.

Wall, Joe L. *Going for the Gold.* Chicago: Moody Press, 1991.

Walvoord, John F. (Ed.) *Chafer's Systematic Theology*, Volume Two. Wheaton: Victor Books, 1988.

Walvoord, John F. *Major Bible Prophecies.* Grand Rapids: Zondervan Publishing House, 1991.

Walvoord, John F. *The Millennial Kingdom.* Grand Rapids: Zondervan Publishing House, 1959.

Walvoord, John F. *The Revelation of Jesus Christ.* Chicago: Moody Press, 1966.

More from Dawson McAllister and Shepherd Ministries...